REAL MAN

MAJORING IN MEN™
The Curriculum for Men

Edwin Louis Cole

watercolor books®

Southlake, Texas

Cover design by Mick Thurber

First printing
ISBN 1931682-23-2

Ed Cole™ Library
P.O. Box 92921
Southlake, TX 76092

www.EdColeLibrary.org

Published by Watercolor Books®
P. O. Box 93234
Southlake, TX 76092
www.watercolorbooks.com

TABLE OF CONTENTS

INTRODUCTION

Welcome aboard! I am delighted to extend greetings on behalf of men from Cincinnati to Singapore, and from New York to Nepal, who are stepping up to the challenge of MAJORING IN MEN™.

My prayer, as you work through this book, is for God to reveal Himself and yourself, pinpointing areas of your life for change and encouraging you in your strengths, convictions and dreams.

Some men will skim through and receive some help. Others—and I trust this means you—will read the books, meditate on the truths and memorize the principles, all with the ambition of becoming great men of courage, mighty men of valor—the heroes desperately needed in today's world.

My goal is for you to be changed, educated and, most of all, deepened in conviction and revelation that comes only from drawing close to God. My dream in preparing this course is for men to rise up throughout the world to study further, teach better and reach more men than I have. To that end and for that purpose, I have devoted my life and labor for the last fifty years.

This may well be one of the most life-changing experiences of your life. Let it be. Better yet—make it be. Truth is like soap. It works only if it's applied.

I admire you for taking this step.

Statement of Ministry

"I have been called to speak with a prophetic voice to the men of this generation and commissioned with a ministry majoring in men to declare a standard for manhood, and that standard is 'manhood and Christlikeness are synonymous.'"

Edwin Louis Cole

"Rules of the Road"
for MAJORING IN MEN™ Curriculum

1. **Give it your all!** This curriculum is a private meeting between your heart and God's. What you put into it determines what you'll get out of it. Give God the opportunity to build character, instill dreams and visions and change your life!

2. **Buy the corresponding book** from your local bookstore. If you cannot find the book locally, you may write to Watercolor Books® at P.O. Box 93234, Southlake, TX 76092, USA, or to order with a credit card by email, log onto www.EdColeLibrary.org.

3. **Take the Self Test** after completing each lesson, using your book as needed. At the end of the book, take the Final Exam.

4. Many churches use MAJORING IN MEN™ curriculum and collect the Final Exams to "graduate" their students. Contact www.EdColeLibrary.org for a list of ministries that commission men.

5. **Let's get going!**

The Masculinity Crisis &
The Substitute Society

Lesson 1
The Masculinity Crisis & The Substitute Society

I.   The Masculinity Crisis (Chapter 1)

    A.   We have a crisis in _____ and in _____. *(page 5)*

       1.   In articles, men are routinely criticized for not spending time with family, etc. In the workplace, men are to behave aggressively, make the sale, create the new project, win the contract. Average men try to cope with these conflicting messages by _____ _____. They end up _____ their identity. *(page 7)*

       2.   People are motivated by what they think is important in this world, whether or not that perception is true. *(page 7)* ___ True ___ False

       3.   Where is the essence of real manhood found? *(circle one)* *(page 8)*
          a.   in how he looks   b.   in who he is   c.   in what he does

       4.   What is the answer for the masculinity crisis? *(page 8)*

          _____

For Further Study
"For as he thinks in his heart, so is he" Proverbs 23:7 AMP.
"Keep thy heart with all diligence; for out of it are the issues of life" Proverbs 4:23.
Moral cowardice causes men to shrink from duty and danger, to dread pain and to yield to fear – 1 Samuel 15:24.
The fear of man is a form of moral cowardice – Proverbs 29:25; Moral cowardice is the ruin of manhood – Numbers 13:33.

B.   Real manhood is found within _____. *(page 10)*

    1.   God is interested in the "inner man," his moral character. *(page 10)*   ___ True ___ False

    2.   Read: *"The spirit of man is the candle of the Lord, searching all the inward parts of the belly"* Proverbs 20:27.

    3.   The quality of a product depends on: *(circle one) (page 11)*
       a.   the value of the producer   b.   the quality of the material used   c.   the market

    4.   The cheaper the merchandise: *(circle one) (page 11)*
       a.   the more you need to pray   b.   the weaker the market   c.   the higher the gloss

    5.   Give some examples of areas where these principles are true. *(page 12)*

      _____

C.   Every man is limited in life by three things: *(page 13)*

    1.   _____

    2.   _____

    3.   _____

For Further Study

The story of the bramble, as an example of weak men ascending to leadership – Judges 9:7-15

Truth is not an option in life – Zechariah 8:16. Truth is the bedrock of integrity. Your personal integrity is the cornerstone of your character – Psalm 24:4, 5.

Moral courage enables a person to encounter hatred, disapproval and contempt without departing from what is right – Psalm 119:157. Examples: Gideon – Judges 6, 7; David – 1 Samuel 17; Daniel – Daniel 6; John the Baptist – Matthew 14:3-10; Stephen – Acts 7; Paul – Acts 27; 28:1-6

D.   Private philosophy determines _____. *(page 14)*

E.   Charm is the _____ and deals with the _____.

Character is _____ and deals with the _____. *(pages 14-15)*

F.   Life is composed of our _____, constructed by our _____ and revealed by our

_____. *(page 15)*

II.   The Substitute Society (Chapter 2)

A.   Substituting _____ values for _____ in _____

can be devastating. *(page 18)*

1.   Define the 1960's teaching method called "Values Clarification." *(page 19)*

_____

_____

For Further Study

Abraham's and Lot's decisions – Genesis 13; 19
Integrity – Firm adherence to a code of especially moral values; Incorruptibility (Dictionary definition)
"I beg you ... to live and act in a way worthy of those who have been chosen for such wonderful blessings as these" Ephesians 4:1 TLB.
Giving cannot be a substitute for obedience – 1 Samuel 15:22; Proverbs 21:27.

2. Many of those caught up in our substitute society are claiming that bad is good and good is bad. In doing so, they try to: *(circle all that apply)* *(page 20-21)*

    a. live a lie rather than embrace truth

    b. justify their inconsistencies

    c. make God into their own image rather than conform to His image

3. Read: *"Woe unto them that call evil good, and good evil; that put darkness for light, and light for darkness; that put bitter for sweet, and sweet for bitter!"* Isaiah 5:20.

B. Those of us who want to be real men must seek to live on a higher level and recognize these

    _____ tendencies, bracing ourselves with _____ and

    _____. *(page 22)*

1. Read: *"He will completely fool those who are on their way to hell because they have said 'no' to the Truth; they have refused to believe it and love it, and let it save them, so God will allow them to believe lies with all their heart, and all of them will be justly judged for believing falsehood, refusing the Truth, and enjoying their sins"* 2 Thessalonians 2:10-12 TLB.

For Further Study

Bad is good or good is bad – *"Why boastest thou thyself in mischief, O mighty man? the goodness of God endureth continually"* Psalm 52:1; Proverbs 17:15; *"Because that, when they knew God, they glorified him not as God, neither were thankful; but became vain in their imaginations, and their foolish heart was darkened. Professing themselves to be wise, they became fools, And changed the glory of the uncorruptible God into an image made like to corruptible man, and to birds, and fourfooted beasts, and creeping things. Wherefore God also gave them up to uncleanness through the lusts of their own hearts, to dishonour their own bodies between themselves"* Romans 1:21-24; Romans 8:29; *"For John the Baptist came neither eating bread nor drinking wine; and ye say, He hath a devil. The Son of man is come eating and drinking; and ye say, Behold a gluttonous man, and a winebibber, a friend of publicans and sinners!"* Luke 7:33-34.

2. Men make substitutions in the most intimate parts of their lives, their _____. What are the two discussed? *(page 23)*

    a. _____   b. _____

3. The Church has also made substitutions. Name six areas. *(page 23)*

    a. _____

    b. _____

    c. _____

    d. _____

    e. _____

    f. _____

C. Many religious people are simply _____ to the Word of God. This is often a form of _____. *(page 24)*

D. What is perhaps the greatest substitution error in the Church? *(page 25)* _____

_____

_____

E. Society is hooked on substitutes; real men go for the real thing, _____. *(page 25)*

For Further Study

Love and obedience, not religious ritual – *"Greater love hath no man than this, that a man lay down his life for his friends"* John 15:13; *"Now I rejoice, not that ye were made sorry, but that ye sorrowed to repentance: for ye were made sorry after a godly manner, that ye might receive damage by us in nothing. For godly sorrow worketh repentance to salvation not to be repented of: but the sorrow of the world worketh death. For behold this selfsame thing, that ye sorrowed after a godly sort, what carefulness it wrought in you, yea, what clearing of yourselves, yea, what indignation, yea, what fear, yea, what vehement desire, yea, what zeal, yea, what revenge! In all things ye have approved yourselves to be clear in this matter"* 2 Corinthians 7:9-11.

"If ye love me, keep my commandments" John 14:15.

"So they come as though they are sincere and sit before you listening. But they have no intention of doing what I tell them to; they talk very sweetly about loving the Lord, but with their hearts they are loving their money" Ezekiel 33:31 TLB; *"But be ye doers of the word, and not hearers only, deceiving your own selves"* James 1:22.

Practical:

1. Read: 2 Timothy 4:3-4 and Ezekiel 33:32. What are these verses saying about society? About you? What can you do to protect yourself and your family from the "substitute society"?

    _____

    _____

    _____

2. In what ways has your own masculinity been "emasculated" (or weakened)? What can you do this week

    to strengthen yourself? _____

    _____

    _____

Repeat this prayer out loud:

Father, in Jesus' Name, I know that I, too, come from a weakened state of manhood, and I need to be filled with Your power and strength. I admit my failures in following society, and I commit myself today to live as a Christ-like man. Thank You for receiving me and my manhood. Amen.

For Further Study

"Not every one that saith unto me, Lord, Lord, shall enter into the kingdom of heaven; but he that doeth the will of my Father which is in heaven" Matthew 7:21.

Substitutions – *"So Shishak king of Egypt came up against Jerusalem, and took away the treasures of the house of the Lord, and the treasures of the king's house; he took all: he carried away also the shields of gold which Solomon had made. Instead of which king Rehoboam made shields of brass, and committed them to the hands of the chief of the guard, that kept the entrance of the king's house. And when the king entered into the house of the Lord, the guard came and fetched them, and brought them again into the guard chamber. And when he humbled himself, the wrath of the Lord turned from him, that he would not destroy him altogether: and also in Judah things went well"* 2 Chronicles 12:9-12.

"And I will give them a heart to recognize, understand and be acquainted with Me, that I am the Lord; and they shall be My people and I will be their God, for they shall return to Me with their whole heart" Jeremiah 24:7 AMP.

Self Test *Lesson 1*

1. The quality of the product depends on the quality of _____ used.

    The cheaper the merchandise, the higher the _____.

2. Name the three things that limit every man in life.

    a. _____

    b. _____

    c. _____

3. Give a short meaning of what the Parable of the Bramble Bush illustrates. _____

    _____

    _____

4. _____ determines public performance.

5. What is the only thing left after the charm wears off? _____

6. Fame can come in a moment, but greatness comes with: *(circle one)*

    a. longevity   b. pain   c. a price tag

7. Name two ways men make substitutions in the intimate parts of their lives.

    a. _____   b. _____

8. The image lie. One problem contributing to the crisis in men today is the reward system offered for

    presenting a great exterior. What are some problems that arise through this thinking? _____

    _____

    _____

    _____

9. In a substitute society, what has society substituted for absolutes? _____

10. What are some areas in which the Church has been guilty of substitution? _____

    _____

    _____

Lesson 2

Cracks in the Mirror &
Behold the Man

Lesson 2
Cracks in the Mirror & Behold the Man

I.   Cracks in the Mirror (Chapter 3)

   A.   A man can go for the image or the stuff of life behind the image. The results are a _____

   man or a _____. *(page 26)*

   B.   Name three identities a man has to deal with. *(page 26)*

   1.   _____

   2.   _____

   3.   _____

   C.   Why was it important for the Lord to magnify Moses' successor, Joshua, in front of Israel? *(page 28)*

   _____

   _____

   D.   Which of the following popular "buzzwords" in business advertising require character to live up to?
   (circle one) (page 29)

   1.   integrity   2.   you deserve this   3.   new!   4.   individual rights

For Further Study

"But we all, with open face beholding as in a glass the glory of the Lord, are changed into the same image from glory to glory, even as by the Spirit of the Lord" 2 Corinthians 3:18.

"On that day the Lord magnified Joshua in the sight of all Israel; and they feared him, as they feared Moses, all the days of his life" Joshua 4:14.

Integrity – *"The just man walketh in his integrity"* Proverbs 20:7. Honesty is the core of integrity – Proverbs 11:3, 5. Counselors determine the destiny of kings – 2 Samuel 16:23; 1 Kings 14.

As disciples, it is our right to know the truth – John 8:31, 32. Learn to discern between good and evil, the truth and a lie – 1 Kings 3:9. Don't be moved by every person's personality, persuasion and belief – Ephesians 4:14. *"Stop listening to teaching that contradicts what you know is right"* Proverbs 19:27 TLB; *"Only a simpleton believes what he is told! A prudent man checks to see where he is going"* Proverbs 14:15 TLB; *"And let the peace ... from Christ rule (act as umpire continually) in your hearts"* Colossians 3:15 AMP; *"But you have received the Holy Spirit and he lives within you, in your hearts ... he teaches you all things, and he is the Truth"* 1 John 2:27 TLB.

E.   What truth about "counsel" is found in the history of Rehoboam and Jeroboam?   *(page 30)*

_____

F.   Use the following words to complete the sentences below: *(pages 31-33)*

identity   virtue   imagine   renew   create

1.   We are motivated to become what we _____ ourselves to be.

2.   The most powerful thing a man can do is _____ an image.

3.   The _____ crisis must be resolved to reach maturity.

4.   To think correctly, you must _____ your mind through the Word of God.

5.   Men and nations are not great by virtue of their wealth but by the wealth of their _____.

G.   How can we resist false images of ourselves?   *(page 32)* _____

_____

H.   Image-makers are powerful today. What does God want us to understand about image?   *(page 33)*

_____

_____

I.   A man's _____ are the expression of his nature.   *(page 33)*

1.   Our words say volumes about our _____.   *(page 33)*

2.   Why was Esau a "profane person"?   *(page 33-34)* _____

_____

_____

For Further Study

"*Of whom a man is overcome, of the same is he brought in bondage*" 2 Peter 2:19.

Base your life on the Word – "*In the beginning was the Word, and the Word was with God, and the Word was God*" John 1:1; "*Who being the brightness of his glory, and the express image of his person, and upholding all things by the word of his power, when he had by himself purged our sins, sat down on the right hand of the Majesty on high*" Hebrews 1:3.

"*Who is the image of the invisible God, the firstborn of every creature*" Colossians 1:15

"*Thou shalt not take the name of the Lord thy God in vain; for the Lord will not hold him guiltless that taketh his name in vain*" Exodus 20:7.

"*Lest there be any fornicator, or profane person, as Esau, who for one morsel of meat sold his birthright*" Hebrews 12:16.

3. Moral character emanates from the _____ of a man's being. *(page 33)*

J. God desires us to: *(circle one)* *(page 34)*

1. cover our nature by projecting an image we want others to believe.

2. have our nature changed by identifying ourselves with the person of Jesus Christ.

3. have our nature changed by what others say about us.

K. Read: *"Above all else, guard your heart, for it is the wellspring of life"* Proverbs 4:23 NIV.

II. Behold the Man (Chapter 4)

A. How long did Jesus prepare for ministry? *(page 37)* _____

1. _____ is the virtue of preparation. *(page 37)*

2. What are some truths we should derive from this aspect of Jesus' life? *(page 37)*

_____

_____

_____

3. Though a Man of grace and gentleness, Jesus' acute sense of right and wrong made Him _____ to rebuke those deserving condemnation. *(page 38)*

4. Jesus was not afraid of controversy. The splendor of His person was such that no man _____ _____. *(page 38)*

For Further Study

Personality is after the outward man and is temporal; it is not the same as character – 1 Samuel 16:7; Proverbs 26:23. Character and the honor of God – obedience to His Word honors God; disobedience dishonors Him – 1 Samuel 15:22-23; Proverbs 14:2. A man who honors God privately will show good character in his decisions – Psalm 119:101-104. God commits to character, not talent – 2 Timothy 2:2; Matthew 25:21; Luke 16:10. Becoming Christlike – Christ's humility – Deuteronomy 8:2-3, 16; 2 Chronicles 7:14; Proverbs 15:33; Philippians 2:1-11; James 4:10; 1 Peter 5:5-6. Christ's ministry of reconciliation – *"And all things are of God, who hath reconciled us to himself by Jesus Christ, and hath given to us the ministry of reconciliation"* 2 Corinthians 5:18. The Christian's purpose – *"Go ye therefore, and teach all nations, baptizing them in the name of the Father, and of the Son, and of the Holy Ghost"* Matthew 28:19; Mark 16:15. Christ's Kingdom – John 18:36

B.   What was Jesus' greatest source of preparation? *(page 38)* _____

Read: *"And all they in the synagogue, when they heard these things, were filled with wrath, And rose up, and thrust him out of the city, and led him unto the brow of the hill whereon their city was built, that they might cast him down headlong. But he passing through the midst of them went his way"* Luke 4:28-30.

C.   Jesus' _____ knew no bounds. His _____ knew no limits. *(page 40)*

D.   Jesus taught that a man is only qualified to lead to the degree that he is _____

_____. *(page 40)*

   1.   True _____ is realized in true humility. *(page 40)*

   2.   What is the essence of humility? _____ *(page 40)*

E.   In looking at the great men of history, what did Jesus do that none of them were able to? *(page 41)*

_____

_____

Practical:
   1.   Read: Philippians 1:1-11.
   2.   Read: *"In him was life; and the life was the light of men"* John 1:4.

Repeat this prayer out loud:

Lord, I accept what I've learned in this lesson. Please reveal to me every area of my life that does not live up to the image of Christ, so I can repent and start fresh in light of what You're teaching me. Please help me commit these principles to my memory and hide them in my heart. In Jesus' Name, I pray, Amen.

For Further Study

Lead by serving – *"But it shall not be so among you: but whosoever will be great among you, let him be your minister; And whosoever will be chief among you, let him be your servant: Even as the Son of man came not to be ministered unto, but to minister, and to give his life a ransom for many"* Matthew 20:26-28.
Christ suffering injustice – *"And he said, Verily I say unto you, No prophet is accepted in his own country. But he passing through the midst of them went his way"* Luke 4:24, 30; John 19:6; Matthew 27:24.
The Christ life – *"In him was life; and the life was the light of men"* John 1:4; Not a life of religious servitude – Matthew 21:12; 23:13-33; John 8:7, 11
Christ's prayer life – Luke 6:12-13; 22:39-46; Christ's compassion – Matthew 25:40

Self Test *Lesson 2*

1. What is the difference between a "fabricated" man and a real man?

    a. _____

    _____

    b. _____

    _____

2. What are three identities a man has to deal with?

    a. _____

    b. _____

    c. _____

3. A man's true integrity is found in: *(circle one)*

    a. his company worth   b. his ideal of himself   c. his personal character

4. What connection was made between "counselors" and "kings"?

    _____

5. We are motivated to become what we _____ ourselves to be.

6. The most powerful thing a man can do is create an image.   ___ True   ___ False

7. To think correctly, you must _____ your mind through the Word of God.

8. Men and nations are great by virtue of their wealth.   ___ True   ___ False

9. Jesus had thirty years of preparation for three years of ministry. What is one truth we see through this?

    _____

10. What is the greatest thing Jesus did to prepare for ministry? _____

11. What did Jesus do to assure Himself of right decisions? _____

    Is this pattern right for us? _____

12. A man is only qualified to lead to the degree that he is _____.

13. True nobility comes from _____.

14. John 1:4 says, "*In Him was* _____*; and the* _____ *was the light of men.*"

Lesson 3

The Power of Life &
Life-Changing Values

Lesson 3
The Power of Life & Life-Changing Values

I.   The Power of Life (Chapter 5)

    A.   Draw a line between phrases to create four basic principles. *(page 42)*

        1. Communication is the   a. key to life

        2. Exchange is the   b. power of life

        3. Balance is the   c. process of life

        4. Agreement is the   d. basis of life

    B.   _____ doesn't make the man; it only exposes a man for what he is. *(page 43)*

        1. The only constant in maturity is _____. *(page 43)*

        2. Change customarily produces _____. *(page 43)*

    C.   Name some forms of death. *(page 43-44)*

        1. _____   3. _____   5. _____

        2. _____   4. _____   6. _____

For Further Study

Reliable communication – *"Reliable communication permits progress"* Proverbs 13:17 TLB; Mark 4:11-12, 23-24.
Rules for communication – With others – *"Wherefore, my beloved brethren, let every man be swift to hear, slow to speak, slow to wrath"* James 1:19; With wives – *"Husbands, dwell with them according to knowledge, giving honour unto the wife, as unto the weaker vessel, and as being heirs together of the grace of life; that your prayers be not hindered"* 1 Peter 3:7; With children – *"And ye fathers, provoke not your children to wrath: but nurture them in the chastening and admonition of the Lord"* Ephesians 6:4.
Agreement – Genesis 11:6; Exodus 13:18; Amos 3:3; *"If two of you shall agree on earth as touching any thing that they shall ask, it shall be done for them of my Father which is in heaven"* Matthew 18:19; Every city or house divided against itself shall not stand – Matthew 12:25.

D. Fill in the blanks to complete eight propositions concerning death. *(pages 44-45)*

1. To the Christian, death is only a _____ from one state of being to another that is _____.

2. Death is only an _____ when it occurs outside of _____.

3. Any death in Christ must be followed by a _____ or it is not in Christ.

4. The resurrection is the ultimate _____.

5. Jesus established a principle when He said, *"He that findeth his _____ shall lose it: and he that loseth his _____ for my sake shall find it"* Matthew 10:39.

6. For the Christian, there are many forms of dying to _____.

7. _____ death can occur in many ways, but in many countries, it is mitigated by _____ laws.

8. There is death, and there is a "_____ of _____."

E. Name the fivefold temptations men like Elijah suffer. *(page 46)*

1. _____   4. _____

2. _____   5. _____

3. _____

For Further Study

Death in Christ – *"For this corruptible must put on incorruption, and this mortal must put on immortality. So when this corruptible shall have put on incorruption, and this mortal shall have put on immortality, then shall be brought to pass the saying that is written, Death is swallowed up in victory"* 1 Corinthians 15:53-54; 1 Corinthians 3:22; Matthew 10:39.

Temptation – *"Then was Jesus led up of the Spirit into the wilderness to be tempted of the devil. And when he had fasted forty days and forty nights, he was afterward an hungered. And when the tempter came to him, he said, If thou be the Son of God ... Then saith Jesus unto him, Get thee hence, Satan: for it is written, Thou shalt worship the Lord thy God, and him only shalt thou serve. Then the devil leaveth him, and, behold, angels came and ministered unto him"* Matthew 4:1-11; Romans 4:25.

Elijah's ordeal – 1 Kings 18-19

F.   Failing is not the worst thing in the world. What is? _____ *(page 47)*

G.   What is the real secret to success in ministry, life and marriage? *(page 49)*

_____

H.   Death and resurrection go together. The _____ and the _____ are incomplete without one another. *(page 49)*

II.   Life-Changing Values (Chapter 6)

A.   Use the following words to fill in the characteristics God gave man to live a Christ-like life. *(page 51)*

will   words   moral excellence   reproduce   truth

1.   Capacity to know _____

2.   Ability to recognize _____

3.   Power to exercise our _____

4.   Creative power in our _____

5.   Right and ability to _____

For Further Study

Death and resurrection – *"For the good that I would I do not: but the evil which I would not, that I do"* Romans 7:19; *"For the law of the Spirit of life in Christ Jesus hath made me free from the law of sin and death"* Romans 8:2; Luke 22:41-44; *"The thief cometh not, but for to steal, and to kill, and to destroy: I am come that they might have life, and that they might have it more abundantly"* John 10:10.

Never quit – *"Brethren, I count not myself to have apprehended: but this one thing I do, forgetting those things which are behind, and reaching forth unto those things which are before, I press toward the mark for the prize of the high calling of God in Christ Jesus"* Philippians 3:13-14.

"Yea, a man may say, Thou hast faith, and I have works: shew me thy faith without thy works, and I will shew thee my faith by my works" James 2:18.

B. Name three differences between "preference" and "conviction." *(page 55)*

　　1. Convictions are _____.

　　2. Under pressure, convictions grow _____.

　　3. People who live by preference always dislike those who hold _____.

C. Fill in the blanks to complete these eight propositions concerning life's value systems.

　　1. Some things in life are more important than _____. *(page 55)*

　　2. The _____ is more important than the _____. *(page 57)*

　　3. Money clarifies your _____. *(page 60)*

　　4. Whoever dictates your _____ becomes your _____. *(page 61)*

　　5. Individual _____ cannot exceed the corporate _____. *(page 62)*

　　6. Fathers provide the family's _____. *(page 63)*

　　7. Values can be _____ then _____. *(page 64)*

　　8. Everything in life has _____. *(page 65)*

For Further Study

Preferences – *"For Demas hath forsaken me, having loved this present world, and is departed unto Thessalonica"* 2 Timothy 4:10; *"And Esau came from the field, and he was faint: And Esau said to Jacob, Feed me, I pray thee, with that same red pottage; for I am faint … And Jacob said, Sell me this day thy birthright. And Esau said, Behold, I am at the point to die: and what profit shall this birthright do to me? … thus Esau despised his birthright"* Genesis 25:29-34; *"But it is happened unto them according to the true proverb, The dog is turned to his own vomit again; and the sow that was washed to her wallowing in the mire"* 2 Peter 2:22.
Convictions – *"Esteeming the reproach of Christ greater riches than the treasures in Egypt: for he had respect unto the recompence of the reward"* Hebrews 11:26; Daniel 3, 6; 2 Chronicles 16:9; *"For Herod had laid hold on John, and bound him, and put him in prison for Herodias' sake, his brother Philip's wife. For John said unto him, It is not lawful for thee to have her … And he sent, and beheaded John in the prison"* Matthew 14:3-11.

D.   When a man claims his value system is his own, he becomes his own _____. *(page 62)*

1.   It's the _____ responsibility to provide a family's value system. *(page 63)*

2.   What is the biblical pattern for the discipleship of the family? *(page 64)* _____

_____

3.   The greatest value of a father's legacy is the _____ he leaves in his child's life. *(page 64)*

E.   Timing is the _____ in success. *(page 65)*

1.   Time has _____ value.   3.   Time spent is _____.

2.   Time wasted is _____.   4.   Time invested is _____.

For Further Study

Valuing the internal – *"While we look not at the things which are seen, but at the things which are not seen: for the things which are seen are temporal; but the things which are not seen are eternal"* 2 Corinthians 4:18.

Valuing your name and reputation – *"A good name is rather to be chosen than great riches, and loving favour rather than silver and gold"* Proverbs 22:1.

Valuing things – *"And through covetousness shall they with feigned words make merchandise of you: whose judgment now of a long time lingereth not, and their damnation slumbereth not"* 2 Peter 2:3.

Valuing God's Word – *"I have heard what the prophets said, that prophesy lies in my name, saying, I have dreamed, I have dreamed"* Jeremiah 23:25.

Practical:

1. Jesus' motivation was love for the Father. His mission was to seek and save the lost. His ministry is as our "Prophet, Priest and King." *(page 56)* How do you believe these would parallel the motivation,

    mission and ministry of a real man? _____

    _____

Repeat this prayer out loud:

Father God, I reject the spirit of death that would try to defeat me. I appropriate the blood of Jesus over those "dead" areas of my life and believe You for a resurrection through Christ. Regardless of what others do, I choose to be a man of conviction, nor preference—the right man, at the right time, in the right place. Amen.

For Further Study

Valuing others – *"I am the good shepherd: the good shepherd giveth his life for the sheep"* John 10:11.
Valuing Christian leaders – *"Let the elders that rule well be counted worthy of double honour, especially they who labour in the word and doctrine"* 1 Timothy 5:17.
Valuing money – *"For where your treasure is, there will your heart be also"* Luke 12:34.
Protecting against others' poor values and preferences – *"Your glorying is not good. Know ye not that a little leaven leaveneth the whole lump? But now I have written unto you not to keep company, if any man that is called a brother be a fornicator, or covetous, or an idolater, or a railer, or a drunkard, or an extortioner; with such an one no not to eat"* 1 Corinthians 5:6, 11; *"A little leaven leaveneth the whole lump"* Galatians 5:9.

Self Test *Lesson 3*

1. What are the four principles in life every man needs to understand?

    a. Communication is the _____.   c. Balance is the _____.

    b. Exchange is the _____.   d. Agreement is the _____.

2. The only constant in maturity is _____.

3. Dying physically is the only form of death.   ___ True ___ False

4. What must any "death" in Christ be followed by? _____

5. Failing is the worst thing in the world that can happen to a man.   ___ True ___ False

6. What does lower morality lead to? _____

7. Under pressure, convictions grow _____.

8. Who provides the family's value system? _____

9. What is the essential ingredient in success? _____

10. Name three forms of dying to self.   a. _____   b. _____   c. _____

11. In Paul's time, what was a possible punishment for someone convicted of deliberately plotting murder?

    _____

12. Convictions are to be negotiable.   ___ True ___ False

13. Fill in the following as they refer to Jesus Christ:

    a. His basic motivation was _____.

    b. His mission was _____.

    c. His ministry is _____.

14. Whoever dictates your values becomes your: *(circle one)*

    a. friend   b. employer   c. god

15. Leaders _____ to influence; followers _____ to influence.

Lesson 4

Maximizing Your Resources &
Staying on Top

Lesson 4
Maximizing Your Resources & Staying on Top

I.   Maximizing Your Resources (Chapter 7)

    A.   As men, we are _____ first and foremost. *(page 69)*

        1.   We do not own what we do not _____. Our _____ are not

            ours to keep, but rather ours to _____ and _____. *(page 69)*

        2.   What are some areas of life where we have been guilty of poor stewardship? *(pages 70)*

            _____

    B.   Ministers do not own the ministry they are in; they are only stewards of the _____ God has given them. *(page 71)*

        1.   Read: *"But anyone who is not aware that he is doing wrong will be punished only lightly. Much is required from those to whom much is given, for their responsibility is greater"* Luke 12:48 TLB.

        2.   What are some reasons ministers/leaders should be careful about "taking succession" into their own

            hands? *(pages 72)* _____

            _____

            _____

For Further Study

Stewards – *"And God said, Let us make man in our image, after our likeness: and let them have dominion over the fish of the sea, and over the fowl of the air, and over the cattle, and over all the earth, and over every creeping thing that creepeth upon the earth"* Genesis 1:26; *"And the Lord God took the man, and put him into the garden of Eden to dress it and to keep it"* Genesis 2:15; *"As every man hath received the gift, even so minister the same one to another, as good stewards of the manifold grace of God"* 1 Peter 4:10.

Succession – *"So Isaac went away from there and pitched his tent in the valley of Gerar, and dwelt there. And Isaac dug again the wells of water which had been dug in the days of Abraham his father, for the Philistines had stopped them after the death of Abraham; and he gave them the names by which his father had called them"* Genesis 26:17-18; *"Better is a poor and a wise child than an old and foolish king, who will no more be admonished"* Ecclesiastes 4:13.

3. What lesson can we learn from Abraham and Isaac regarding succession? *(page 72-73)*

    _____

    _____

4. Sons can inherit ministries, but they cannot inherit _____. *(page 73)*

C. Are the following statements about men and their ministries True or False? *(page 70-74)*

    1. It takes a man to admit he's wrong. ___ True ___ False

    2. The Kingdom of God runs on sentiment. ___ True ___ False

    3. To whom much is given, from him much is required. ___ True ___ False

    4. Ministers own their ministries. ___ True ___ False

    5. Men are stewards of their vote. ___ True ___ False

D. The _____ is the vital force behind the vision of any ministry or business. *(page 73)*

E. God gave Adam a direct charge to _____, _____ and _____, which translates into: _____, _____ and _____. *(page 74)*

II. Staying on Top (Chapter 8)

A. Prayer produces _____. *(page 76)*

For Further Study

Stewardship of: Ministry – *"While I was with them in the world, I kept them in thy name: those that thou gavest me I have kept, and none of them is lost, but the son of perdition; that the scripture might be fulfilled"* John 17:12; Talents – *"But he that knew not, and did commit things worthy of stripes, shall be beaten with few stripes. For unto whomsoever much is given, of him shall be much required: and to whom men have committed much, of him they will ask the more"* Luke 12:48; Wives – *"So ought men to love their wives as their own bodies. He that loveth his wife loveth himself. For no man ever yet hated his own flesh; but nourisheth and cherisheth it, even as the Lord the church"* Ephesians 5:28-29.
Faithfulness – *"Moreover it is required in stewards, that a man be found faithful"* 1 Corinthians 4:2.
Ministry requirements – *"This is a true saying, If a man desire the office of a bishop, he desireth a good work"* 1 Timothy 3:1; Reputation – Ethics – Morality – Temperament – Habits – Maturity

B. Name eleven ways God speaks to men. *(pages 78-79)*

1. His _____

2. An _____

3. _____

4. _____

5. _____

6. Spirit to _____

7. _____

8. _____ counsel

9. _____ of the _____

10. _____

11. _____ of the heart

C. Circle the correct answer that completes each of the following sentences. *(pages 79-81)*

1. God sends a word, gives it _____ and brings healing to the world.

    a. an amplifier   b. a body   c. a church group

2. All God's work begins with His _____.

    a. word   b. power   c. Heaven

3. The pattern of revelation and the process of crystallization follow the _____.

    a. word   b. power   c. obedience of men

4. It is easier to obtain than to _____.

    a. steal   b. maintain   c. give up

For Further Study

God's Word – Matthew 4:4; Deuteronomy 8:3

Audible Voice – Matthew 3:17; 17:5; Acts 9:3-5

Angels – Judges 6:12; Matthew 1:20

Dreams – Genesis 37:5; Matthew 1:20

Visions – Acts 10:10; 26:19; Revelation 1:9-20

Spirit to spirit – Luke 2:26; *"As they ministered to the Lord, and fasted, the Holy Ghost said"* Acts 13:2; *"For as many as are led by the Spirit of God, they are the sons of God … The Spirit itself beareth witness with our spirit, that we are the children of God"* Romans 8:14-16.

Prophets – Luke 1:67-70; Ephesians 2:19-22. *"God, who at sundry times and in divers manners spake in time past unto the fathers by the prophets"* Hebrews 1:1.

Wise Counsel – Acts 5:34; Proverbs 11:14

Desires – *"Delight thyself also in the Lord; and he shall give thee the desires of thine heart"* Psalm 37:4.

5. Revelation inspires change through the _____.

    a. natural progression of evolution   b. expulsive power of a new affection

6. God never explains Himself; He _____ Himself.

    a. announces   b. reveals   c. gets mad at

D. List the pattern and process of revelation and crystallization. *(page 81-82)*

    1. _____   4. _____

    2. _____   5. _____

    3. _____   6. _____

E. Draw a line to match the following. *(page 82)*

    1. The sin of youth   a. pride

    2. The sin of middle age   b. prejudice

    3. The sin of old age   c. passion

F. Read: *"In the beginning God created the heaven and the earth. And the earth was without form, and void; and darkness was upon the face of the deep. And the Spirit of God moved upon the face of the waters. And God said, Let there be light: and there was light"* Genesis 1:1-3.

Read: *"In the beginning was the Word, and the Word was with God, and the Word was God"* John 1:1.

For Further Study

Christ's nature – *"Whereby are given unto us exceeding great and precious promises: that by these ye might be partakers of the divine nature, having escaped the corruption that is in the world through lust"* 2 Peter 1:4; *"Therefore if any man be in Christ, he is a new creature: old things are passed away; behold, all things are become new"* 2 Corinthians 5:17; *"He sent his word, and healed them, and delivered them from their destructions"* Psalm 107:20; Malachi 4:2; John 1:1, 14.

Revelation – *"In the beginning God"* Genesis 1:1-3; *"In the beginning was the Word"* John 1:1. *"The just shall live by faith"* Habakkuk 2:4; Romans 1:17.

Sanctification – *"And the very God of peace sanctify you wholly; and I pray God your whole spirit and soul and body be preserved blameless unto the coming of our Lord Jesus Christ"* 1 Thessalonians 5:23; 2 Corinthians 6:17.

Power – Acts 1:8

Renewal – Romans 12:2; 1 Thessalonians 2:13; Matthew 9:17

G. In relationships, distance is measured by _____, intimacy is measured by _____. The more _____ the application, the more distant the worshiper to the _____. *(page 81)*

H. Institutionalization can be described as men going through the motions without _____. *(pages 82)*

I. What are some identifying factors of being in the area of "crystallization"? *(page 82)*

_____

_____

1. How do men determine the process of "crystallization"? *(page 82)*

_____

2. Where in today's life can we readily see this pattern? *(page 83)*

_____

J. What critical responsibility must all men accept to keep from "crystallization"? *(page 85)*

_____

K. Why did Israel suffer defeat at the battle of Ai? *(page 87)*

_____

For Further Study

Taking the Word to future generations – Joshua 4:4-9; Judges 2:10

Fresh manna – *"And Moses said, Let no man leave of it till the morning. Notwithstanding they hearkened not unto Moses; but some of them left of it until the morning, and it bred worms, and stank: and Moses was wroth with them. And they gathered it every morning, every man according to his eating: and when the sun waxed hot, it melted"* Exodus 16:16-21.

Abiding in Christ – *"I am the vine, ye are the branches: He that abideth in me, and I in him, the same bringeth forth much fruit: for without me ye can do nothing"* John 15:5.

Battle of Ai – Joshua 6-7

Three basic sins – *"And when the woman saw that the tree was good for food, and that it was pleasant to the eyes, and a tree to be desired to make one wise, she took of the fruit thereof, and did eat, and gave also unto her husband with her; and he did eat"* Genesis 3:6.

L.   How does God meet the needs of contemporary society? *(page 87)*

_____

Practical:

1.   Discuss what is meant by "the more a man serves, the greater he becomes." *(page 75)*

2.   Think about your place of work. Fill in what person or department fills these roles:

   Visionary _____

   Administrator _____

   Ruler _____

3.   At what point in the process of crystallization are you in each of these areas?
   (not necessary to write out)

   marriage   children   career   Christian walk

Repeat this prayer out loud:

Father, I repent for not leading by serving others. I repent for not seeking fresh revelation. I ask, in the Name of Jesus, for help in becoming the man You created me to be in every area of my life. I set my face like flint toward the image of Christ-likeness. You are teaching me, and I refuse to be discouraged! Amen.

For Further Study

Abiding fresh in Christ – *"Love not the world, neither the things that are in the world. If any man love the world, the love of the Father is not in him. For all that is in the world, the lust of the flesh, and the lust of the eyes, and the pride of life, is not of the Father, but is of the world. And the world passeth away, and the lust thereof: but he that doeth the will of God abideth for ever"* 1 John 2:15-17; *"Abide in me, and I in you … I am the vine, ye are the branches: He that abideth in me, and I in him, the same bringeth forth much fruit: for without me ye can do nothing … If ye abide in me, and my words abide in you, ye shall ask what ye will, and it shall be done unto you. Herein is my Father glorified, that ye bear much fruit; so shall ye be my disciples … If ye keep my commandments, ye shall abide in my love; even as I have kept my Father's commandments, and abide in his love"* John 15:4-10; *"If ye abide in me, and my words abide in you, ye shall ask what ye will, and it shall be done unto you"* John 17:7.

Self Test *Lesson 4*

1. Man has been given what three basic responsibilities?

   a. _____ b. _____ c. _____

2. Anything we actually possess, we own. ___ True ___ False

3. The Kingdom of God runs on sentiment. ___ True ___ False

4. Abraham's sons inherited his ministry, but each had to do what? _____

5. Who is the real force behind a vision? _____

6. What is the least a real man must do if he has the power to vote? *(circle one)*

   a. vote   b. help back candidates   c. go into politics

7. Name four ways God speaks to us today.

   a. _____ c. _____

   b. _____ d. _____

8. Name the six major steps of the Pattern of Revelation.

   a. _____ d. _____

   b. _____ e. _____

   c. _____ f. _____

9. Prejudice is the sin of: *(circle one)*

   a. middle age   b. youth   c. old age

10. To keep a marriage from becoming "crystallized," what must a man do?

    _____

    _____

11. What is God's "large-scope" pattern? _____

    _____

12. God is a God of perpetuity. Write a short definition of this description of God.

    _____

    _____

Lesson 5

The Cornerstone of Character &
Nothing but the Truth

-

Lesson 5
The Cornerstone of Character & Nothing but the Truth

I.   The Cornerstone of Character (Chapter 9)

    A.   Faithfulness – The Cornerstone

        1.   Read: *"And the things that thou hast heard of me among many witnesses, the same commit thou to faithful men, who shall be able to teach others also"* 2 Timothy 2:2.

        2.   How would the error of transposition make this Scripture read? *(page 89)*

        _____

        3.   _____ is the cornerstone of character. *(page 89)*

        4.   In the Parable of the Talents, we see taught the "Law of Capital" or the "Law of Increase and Decline." What is the basic definition of this? *(page 90)* _____

        _____

        5.   Read: Matthew 25:14-30.

For Further Study

Man's faithfulness – *"And the things that thou hast heard of me among many witnesses, the same commit thou to faithful men, who shall be able to teach others also"* 2 Timothy 2:2; *"He who is faithful in a very little [thing], is faithful also in much; and he who is dishonest and unjust in a very little [thing], is dishonest and unjust also in much"* Luke 16:10; Luke 19:12-27.

God's faithfulness – *"Know therefore that the Lord thy God, he is God, the faithful God, which keepeth covenant and mercy with them that love him and keep his commandments to a thousand generations"* Deuteronomy 7:9; *"Who was faithful to him that appointed him, as also Moses was faithful in all his house"* Hebrews 3:2.

6. What was the sin of the steward who hid his talent? *(page 90)*

_____

7. You can build character in one single defining moment. *(page 91)* ___ True ___ False

B. Indolence and insolence are often the characteristics of the unfaithful.

1. Indolence is _____. *(page 91)*

2. Insolence is passing the _____ on to _____. *(page 91)*

C. Why is it so extremely important to be found faithful with that which is another man's? *(page 92)*

_____

_____

_____

1. How did Elisha qualify himself to receive Elijah's mantle? *(page 92-93)*

_____

_____

For Further Study

The poor steward – *"Then he which had received the one talent came and said, Lord, I knew thee that thou art an hard man … And I was afraid, and went and hid thy talent in the earth … His lord answered and said unto him, Thou wicked and slothful servant, thou knewest that I reap where I sowed not, and gather where I have not strawed: Take therefore the talent from him, and give it unto him which hath ten talents. For unto every one that hath shall be given, and he shall have abundance: but from him that hath not shall be taken away even that which he hath"* Matthew 25:24-26, 28-29.

Qualifying to have your own – *"And if ye have not been faithful in that which is another man's, who shall give you that which is your own?"* Luke 16:12; James 1:22; 2 Kings 3:11; *"And the Lord said unto Moses, Take thee Joshua the son of Nun, a man in whom is the spirit, and lay thine hand upon him"* Numbers 27:18; *"Wherefore, holy brethren, partakers of the heavenly calling, consider the Apostle and High Priest of our profession, Christ Jesus. Who was faithful to him that appointed him, as also Moses was faithful in all his house"* Hebrews 3:1-2.

2.   How did Joshua become qualified to take over leadership from Moses? *(page 93)*

_____

D.   Circle the three essential ingredients in faithfulness. *(page 93-94)*

constancy   diplomacy   leadership   submission   responsibility   loyalty

E.   **In your own words,** define sedition. *(page 94)* _____

_____

1.   What is the solution to sedition? *(page 96)* _____

2.   What does a faithful man do when he's been unfaithful? *(page 98)* _____

For Further Study

Failure in stewardship – Proverbs 11:13; *"Now the works of the flesh are manifest, which are these; Adultery, fornication, uncleanness, lasciviousness, Idolatry, witchcraft, hatred, variance, emulations, wrath, strife, seditions, heresies, Envyings, murders, drunkenness, revellings, and such like"* Galatians 5:19-21; *"Mortify therefore your members which are upon the earth; fornication, uncleanness, inordinate affection, evil concupiscence, and covetousness, which is idolatry"* Colossians 3:5; *"And you hath he quickened, who were dead in trespasses and sins; Wherein in time past ye walked according to the course of this world, according to the prince of the power of the air, the spirit that now worketh in the children of disobedience: Among whom also we all had our conversation in times past in the lusts of our flesh, fulfilling the desires of the flesh and of the mind; and were by nature the children of wrath, even as others. But God, who is rich in mercy, for his great love wherewith he loved us, Even when we were dead in sins, hath quickened us together with Christ, (by grace ye are saved;)"* Ephesians 2:1-5.
The answer to sedition is submission – James 4:7; Ephesians 5:21.

II. Nothing but the Truth (Chapter 10)

A. Truth is mankind's greatest _____ in _____. *(page 99)*

    1. Read: Proverbs 2:1-12.

    2. The more we base our life on truth, the better will be our _____, and the greater will be our _____. *(page 100)*

B. Why can we say "to change the corporate community, the individual must change"? *(page 102)*

_____

_____

C. Why is it right to say that "trust is extended to the limit of truth and no more"? *(pages 103)*

_____

_____

For Further Study

Absalom's rebellion – 2 Samuel 15:1-6; 18:9-15

The prodigal son's rebellion – Luke 15:11-32

Adhering to God's Word – Ezekiel 33:30-33

Jesus is Truth – *"Jesus saith unto him, I am the way, the truth, and the life: no man cometh unto the Father, but by me"* John 14:6; *"And ye shall know the truth, and the truth shall make you free"* John 8:32.

Obstacles to Truth – 2 Corinthians 4:4; *"And judgment is turned away backward, and justice standeth afar off: for truth is fallen in the street, and equity cannot enter"* Isaiah 59:14.

Mingled seed – *"Ye shall keep my statutes. Thou shalt not let thy cattle gender with a diverse kind: thou shalt not sow thy field with mingled seed: neither shall a garment mingled of linen and woollen come upon thee"* Leviticus 19:19.

Partaking of another man's sins – *"Lay hands suddenly on no man, neither be partaker of other men's sins: keep thyself pure"* 1 Timothy 5:22.

D. Name the three basic characteristics of sin. *(page 104)*

1. _____   2. _____   3. _____

E. What was the difference between King David and King Saul? *(105)*

_____

F. A lack of truth leads to a lack of _____. *(page 106)*

1. When a woman can no longer _____ a man because she cannot trust his word,

she no longer wants to _____. *(page 106)*

2. Read: *"... because they did not welcome the Truth but refused to love it that they might be saved. Therefore God sends upon them a misleading influence, a working of error and a strong delusion to make them believe what is false. In order that all may be judged and condemned who did not believe in [who refused to adhere to, trust in, and rely on] the Truth, but [instead] took pleasure in unrighteousness"* 2 Thessalonians 2:10-12 AMP.

3. Our freedom from wrong believing is dependent upon our _____to receive

_____. *(page 108)*

For Further Study

Lack of truth – *"Ye are of your father the devil, and the lusts of your father ye will do. He was a murderer from the beginning, and abode not in the truth, because there is no truth in him. When he speaketh a lie, he speaketh of his own: for he is a liar, and the father of it"* John 8:44; Job 12:11 TLB; 2 Samuel 11-12; *"And Nathan said to David, Thou art the man. Thus saith the Lord God of Israel, I anointed thee king over Israel, and I delivered thee out of the hand of Saul"* 2 Samuel 12:7; Psalm 51; Cost Saul the kingdom – *"But now thy kingdom shall not continue: the Lord hath sought him a man after his own heart, and the Lord hath commanded him to be captain over his people, because thou hast not kept that which the Lord commanded thee"* 1 Samuel 13:5-14.

Truth will be found out – *"Nothing is [so closely] covered up that it will not be revealed, or hidden that it will not be known"* Luke 12:2 AMP; *"But if ye will not do so, behold, ye have sinned against the Lord and be sure your sin will find you out"* Numbers 32:23.

Practical:

1. Think about the sins of sedition. Have you been touched by sedition? As a participant or victim? In what areas of your life do you need to guard against others' sedition? In what areas do you become tempted to take part in sedition?

2. Read: Jesus said, *"I am the way, the truth, and the life: no man cometh unto the Father, but by me"* John 14:6.

3. Determine the correct order of priority: wife   God   ministry   children   career
    How closely do you follow your own convictions of these priorities?

Repeat this prayer out loud:

Father, I come to You like every man, dealing with issues of faithfulness and truthfulness. I ask You to forgive me for every time I've failed in these areas and to help me become more of the man of God You intend for me to be. I accept the forgiveness that is mine through Christ Jesus, my Lord. Amen.

For Further Study

Making things right – *"Therefore if thou bring thy gift to the altar, and there rememberest that thy brother hath ought against thee; Leave there thy gift before the altar, and go thy way; first be reconciled to thy brother, and then come and offer thy gift"* Matthew 5:23-24.
Cherish truth – *"And ye shall know the truth, and the truth shall make you free"* John 8:32; *"Buy the truth, and sell it not; also wisdom, and instruction, and understanding"* Proverbs 23:23.

Self Test *Lesson 5*

1. Faithfulness is the cornerstone of character. What is the significance of a "cornerstone"?

    _____

    _____

    _____

2. We are to find men who are extremely able and give them responsibility. ___ True ___ False

3. Give a definition of the "Law of Capital" spoken of in the Parable of the Talents.

    _____

4. The reward for being trustworthy is _____.

5. To qualify for our own, we must be faithful in that which is _____.

6. What is a common type of treason in homes, businesses and churches? _____

7. Give an illustration of how the sin of sedition works.

    _____

    _____

8. Truth and wisdom can be found merely lying on the surface of life's strata. ___ True ___ False

9. What has to happen before the corporate community can change?

    _____

10. Name the three characteristics of sin.

    a. _____ b. _____ c. _____

11. The Lord warned Israel against mingling their seed with that of foreign nations. We are to keep ourselves pure, according to the New Testament. What does this communicate to us considering our respect of truth?

    _____

    _____

12. Place the following in their correct order of priority.

    Wife   God   Ministry   Children   Career

    1 - _____   2 - _____   3 - _____   4 - _____   5 - _____

Lesson 6

Love or Lust &
Royal Pursuits

Lesson 6
Love or Lust & Royal Pursuits

I.   Love or Lust (Chapter 11)

    A.   Love is the desire to _____ at the expense of _____ because love desires

        to _____. Lust is the desire to _____ at the expense of _____

        because lust desires to _____. *(page 110)*

        1.   Temptation to sin always comes parading the consequences of sin. *(page 110)*
            ___ True ___ False

        2.   There is no pleasure in sin. *(page 111)*   ___ True ___ False

    B.   Sins can be forgiven immediately, but the _____ can last a lifetime. *(page 111)*

        1.   When Satan tempts us, he shows us only the immediate _____. *(page 111)*

        2.   The torment of the temptation to sin is nothing compared with the _____ of the
            _____ of sin. *(page 111)*

        3.   How can we "torment the tempter"? *(page 112)* _____

For Further Study

Love gives – *"For God so loved the world, that he gave"* John 3:16.

Overcoming temptation – *"Choosing rather to suffer affliction with the people of God, than to enjoy the pleasures of sin for a season"* Hebrews 11:25

Sinfulness – *"But before they lay down, the men of the city, even the men of Sodom, compassed the house round, both old and young, all the people from every quarter: And they called unto Lot, and said unto him, Where are the men which came in to thee this night? bring them out unto us, that we may know them"* Genesis 19:4-5; *"Saying, Let us alone; what have we to do with thee, thou Jesus of Nazareth? art thou come to destroy us? I know thee who thou art; the Holy One of God"* Luke 4:34; *"And, behold, they cried out, saying, What have we to do with thee, Jesus, thou Son of God? art thou come hither to torment us before the time?"* Matthew 8:29; *"An unjust man is an abomination to the just: and he that is upright in the way is abomination to the wicked"* Proverbs 29:27.

C. Name some ways in which men lust besides sexual lust. *(page 112)*

_____

D. Are lust and peace compatible? *(page 112)*   ___ Yes ___ No

E. What are the three basic forms of temptations that Jesus and all of mankind face? *(page 113)*

1. _____ 2. _____ 3. _____

F. Read: Luke 4:1-13.

1. How did Jesus overcome the temptations of Satan? *(page 113)*

_____

2. Which of the three forms of temptation is "basic covetousness"? *(page 115)*

_____

G. God's plan for overcoming lust is _____

_____. *(page 119)*

H. Read: *"For the grace of God that bringeth salvation hath appeared to all men, Teaching us that, denying ungodliness and worldly lusts, we should live soberly, righteously, and godly, in this present world"* Titus 2:11-12.

God's grace empowers man to overcome _____. *(pages 119)*

For Further Study

The basic temptations – *"For all that is in the world, the lust of the flesh, and the lust of the eyes, and the pride of life, is not of the Father, but is of the world"* 1 John 2:16; *"And when the woman saw that the tree was good for food, and that it was pleasant to the eyes, and a tree to be desired to make one wise, she took of the fruit thereof, and did eat, and gave also unto her husband with her; and he did eat"* Genesis 3:6.

Judgment – *"And God saw that the wickedness of man was great in the earth, and that every imagination of the thoughts of his heart was only evil continually"* Genesis 6:5; Genesis 19:24-29; Romans 1:26-32.

Purity – *"And this is life eternal, that they might know thee the only true God, and Jesus Christ, whom thou hast sent"* John 17:3; *"The light of the body is the eye: if therefore thine eye be single, thy whole body shall be full of light"* Matthew 6:22; *"The light of the body is the eye: therefore when thine eye is single, thy whole body also is full of light; but when thine eye is evil, thy body also is full of darkness"* Luke 11:34; *"Unto the pure all things are pure: but unto them that are defiled and unbelieving is nothing pure: but even their mind and conscience is defiled"* Titus 1:15.

II. Royal Pursuits (Chapter 12)

   A. Name the two spiritual kingdoms in the world. *(page 121)*

   _____   _____

   1. The characteristics of the kingdom always emanate from the _____

   _____. *(page 122)*

   2. What are some basic characteristic differences between the two kingdoms? *(page 122)*

   _____

   _____

   3. All principles originate in the _____. *(page 122)*

      a. Money follows _____. One thing men need to know is that money has no

         morality; it is amoral, and its morality is determined by the heart of the _____.
         (page 123)

      b. Prayer and production — The physical reciprocal to prayer is _____.

         Prayer precedes _____, but _____ is the

         evidence of _____. *(page 124)*

      c. Spiritual and professional — Seeking first the eternal causes what? *(page 126)*

      _____

For Further Study

Christian living – *"This I say then, Walk in the Spirit, and ye shall not fulfil the lust of the flesh"* Galatians 5:16; *"That ye put off concerning the former conversation the old man, which is corrupt according to the deceitful lusts; And be renewed in the spirit of your mind"* Ephesians 4:22-23; *"My brethren, count it all joy when ye fall into divers temptations"* James 1:2; *"I made a covenant with mine eyes; why then should I think upon a maid?"* Job 31:1.
Kingdom of God – *"Jesus answered and said unto him, Verily, verily, I say unto thee, Except a man be born again, he cannot see the kingdom of God"* John 3:3; *"But seek ye first the kingdom of God, and his righteousness; and all these things shall be added unto you"* Matthew 6:33.
Work as unto the Lord – *"And whatsoever ye do, do it heartily, as to the Lord, and not unto men"* Colossians 3:23; *"For even when we were with you, this we commanded you, that if any would not work, neither should he eat"* 2 Thessalonians 3:10.

B. God's organisms differ from organizations in that they deal with the "political expediency," operate through a _____, make decisions based on _____, accept _____ and attempt to _____. *(page 126)*

C. What is the major difference between "touch" and "method"? *(page 127)* _____
_____

D. In seeking God's Kingdom, what are the five major priorities? *(page 128)*

1. _____   3. _____   5. _____

2. _____   4. _____

Practical:

1. Read: Matthew 6:22 and Job 31:1. What does this mean to how you live your life personally?
_____

2. Remember when you coveted something as a child? Did it pay off? Do you still have it? What can you do today to keep from coveting or wanting things? _____
_____

Repeat this prayer out loud:

Father, I long to seek Your Kingdom first and trust that everything else in life will be added to that. As I work, let money follow. As I pray, let production follow. Help me to say "no" to temptations of all kinds so I can say "yes" to You. In Jesus' Name, I pray. Amen.

For Further Study

Production – *"For who hath despised the day of small things?"* Zechariah 4:10; *"And if it bear fruit, well: and if not, then after that thou shalt cut it down"* Luke 13:9.
"When a man's ways please the Lord, he maketh even his enemies to be at peace with him" Proverbs 16:7.
Abide in Christ – 1 John 2:27; *"If ye abide in me, and my words abide in you, ye shall ask what ye will, and it shall be done unto you"* John 15:7.
Seek the Lord first – Genesis 13:4; *"This book of the law shall not depart out of thy mouth; but thou shalt meditate therein day and night, that thou mayest observe to do according to all that is written therein: for then thou shalt make thy way prosperous, and then thou shalt have good success"* Joshua 1:8; *"But seek ye first the kingdom of God, and his righteousness; and all these things shall be added unto you"* Matthew 6:33.

Self Test *Lesson 6*

1. Define love and lust.

   Love is _____

   _____

   Lust is _____

   _____

2. Which verse in the Bible describes the condition of men "burning" in their lusts? _____

3. Men can be tempted to lust in ways other than sexual. Name several.

   a. _____   c. _____

   b. _____   d. _____

4. What are the three major categories of temptation that come to all men?

   a. _____   c. _____

   b. _____

5. Why is covetousness equal to idolatry? _____

6. How many "spiritual kingdoms" are there? *(circle one)*

   a. too many to count   b. four   c. two

7. How does the money we possess receive morality?

   _____

8. God's provision is always _____, _____ and _____.

   God gives the _____, adds _____, and _____ follows.

9. When God created the Body of Christ, the Church, He created a magnificent organization.

   ___ True ___ False

10. Above all else, the Bible teaches methodology.   ___ True ___ False

11. The closer a man is to God, the more a man of the _____ he becomes.

12. Principles should be instant, but personalities are constants.   ___ True ___ False

Lesson 7

The Cost of Greatness &
The Winning Strategy

Lesson 7
The Cost of Greatness & The Winning Strategy

I.   The Cost of Greatness (Chapter 13)

   A.   What brings maturity? *(page 131)* _____

      1.   Greatness comes through _____. The more you _____, the greater you become. *(page 132)*

      2.   Read: *"Jesus But Jesus called them unto him, and said, Ye know that the princes of the Gentiles exercise dominion over them, and they that are great exercise authority upon them. But it shall not be so among you: but whosoever will be great among you, let him be your minister"* Matthew 20:25-26.

      3.   Mark "T" for True and "F" for False in the following statements: *(pages 132)*

         _____ Jesus' greatness was intensified by His willingness to serve.

         _____ Greatness comes through bossing others around.

         _____ Serving means compensating for what others don't do.

         _____ Companies become great by the number of people they serve.

         _____ Fame and greatness are synonymous.

For Further Study

Serving – *"But it shall not be so among you: but whosoever will be great among you, let him be your minister; And whosoever will be chief among you, let him be your servant: Even as the Son of man came not to be ministered unto, but to minister, and to give his life a ransom for many"* Matthew 20:26-28; John 13:1-17; *"Are they not all ministering spirits, sent forth to minister for them who shall be heirs of salvation?"* Hebrews 1:14; *"And said unto them, Whosoever shall receive this child in my name receiveth me: and whosoever shall receive me receiveth him that sent me: for he that is least among you all, the same shall be great"* Luke 9:48.

Add to your faith – *"And beside this, giving all diligence, add to your faith virtue; and to virtue knowledge; And to knowledge temperance; and to temperance patience; and to patience godliness; And to godliness brotherly kindness; and to brotherly kindness charity"* 2 Peter 1:5-7.

4. The maturation process: To begin with, acceptance of _____ for sin is necessary. What must be handled first for a positive progression to follow? *(page 133)*

   _____

B. What was Adam's major mistake? *(page 133)*

   _____

C. What is a basic tenet of fathering? *(page 134)* _____

   _____

   Children may not always _____ us, but they will always _____ us. *(page 136)*

D. Individually or corporately, what determines greatness of life? *(page 138)*

   _____

E. What is the best measure of your life? *(circle one)* *(page 138)*
   a. prestige   b. power   c. serving   d. fame   e. fortune

For Further Study

Refusing to accept responsibility – *"And the man said, The woman whom thou gavest to be with me, she gave me of the tree, and I did eat"* Genesis 3:12; 1 Samuel 13:11.

Accuser of the brethren – *"And I heard a loud voice saying in heaven, Now is come salvation, and strength, and the kingdom of our God, and the power of his Christ: for the accuser of our brethren is cast down, which accused them before our God day and night"* Revelation 12:10.

Recovery from sinfulness – 1 Samuel 30:1-19; 2 Samuel 12:16-17; *"Who was before a blasphemer, and a persecutor, and injurious: but I obtained mercy, because I did it ignorantly in unbelief. This is a faithful saying, and worthy of all acceptation, that Christ Jesus came into the world to save sinners; of whom I am chief"* 1 Timothy 1:13, 15. *"Pattern after me, follow my example, as I imitate and follow Christ"* 1 Corinthians 11:1 AMP.

Don't seek vengeance – *"I will repay, saith the Lord"* Romans 12:19.

II. The Winning Strategy (Chapter 14)

   A. Define the following: *(page 139)*

     Knowledge: _____

     Understanding: _____

     Wisdom: _____

     Divine wisdom: _____

     Human wisdom: _____

   B. What does the Bible teach us considering wisdom for our future? *(page 140)*

     _____

     _____

   C. Give a definition of the principle "first in intention is last in execution." *(page 141)*

     _____

     _____

For Further Study

"Wisdom is the principal thing; therefore get wisdom: and with all thy getting get understanding" Proverbs 4:7; Proverbs 3:16-17; *"For that they hated knowledge, and did not choose the fear of the Lord: They would none of my counsel: they despised all my reproof"* Proverbs 1:29-31; *"The fear of the Lord is the beginning of knowledge: but fools despise wisdom and instruction"* Proverbs 1:7; Proverbs 23:9; *"The fear of the Lord is the beginning of wisdom"* Psalm 111:10; *"And the spirit of the Lord shall rest upon him, the spirit of wisdom and understanding, the spirit of counsel and might, the spirit of knowledge and of the fear of the Lord"* Isaiah 11:2; *"If any of you lack wisdom, let him ask of God, that giveth to all men liberally, and upbraideth not"* James 1:5; *"This wisdom descendeth not from above, but is earthly, sensual, devilish. But the wisdom that is from above is first pure, then peaceable, gentle, and easy to be intreated, full of mercy and good fruits, without partiality, and without hypocrisy"* James 3:15, 17; *"But of him are ye in Christ Jesus, who of God is made unto us wisdom"* 1 Corinthians 1:30; Ephesians 3:10.

1. The man who has only _____ wisdom invites the devil and the _____ to _____. *(page 141)*

2. Sin is a form of _____. *(page 141)*

D. Write out a definition of "magical thinking." *(page 144)*

_____

_____

E. Name the steps in the pattern for victory. *(page 145)*

   1. _____   3. _____

   2. _____   4. _____

F. Where are strategies developed? *(page 145)* _____

   Where are victories seen? *(page 145)* _____

For Further Study

The wise steward – *"And he said also unto his disciples, There was a certain rich man, which had a steward; and the same was accused unto him that he had wasted his goods. And he called him, and said unto him, How is it that I hear this of thee? give an account of thy stewardship; for thou mayest be no longer steward. Then the steward said within himself, What shall I do? for my lord taketh away from me the stewardship: I cannot dig; to beg I am ashamed. I am resolved what to do, that, when I am put out of the stewardship, they may receive me into their houses. So he called every one of his lord's debtors unto him, and said unto the first, How much owest thou unto my lord? And he said, An hundred measures of oil. And he said unto him, Take thy bill, and sit down quickly, and write fifty. Then said he to another, And how much owest thou? And he said, An hundred measures of wheat. And he said unto him, Take thy bill, and write fourscore. And the lord commended the unjust steward, because he had done wisely: for the children of this world are in their generation wiser than the children of light"* Luke 16:1-8.

Practical:

1. Read: *"Your care for others is the measure of your greatness"* Luke 9:48 TLB.

    Rank your own greatness based on this principle. Place an **"I"** where you would rank yourself, a **"W"** where your wife would rank you, a **"C"** where your children would rank you and an **"E"** for where your employer would rank you.

    1 _____ 5 _____ 10

    little greatness   moderate greatness   great!

2. Why are fame and greatness not the same thing? _____
    _____

3. Give some Biblical examples of great fathering, great leadership and great wisdom.
    _____
    _____

For Further Study

David's strategy for victory – 2 Samuel 5:22-25

Satan's fall – Ezekiel 28:14-17

Magical thinking – *"But Naaman was angry, and went away, and said, Behold, I thought he would surely come out to me, and stand, and call on the name of the Lord his God, and wave his hand over the place, and heal the leper"* 2 Kings 5:11, 13 AMP; *"A man may ruin his chances by his own foolishness and then blame it on the Lord"* Proverbs 19:3 TLB.

Acquire wisdom – *"For wisdom is better than rubies; and all the things that may be desired are not to be compared to it"* Proverbs 8:11; *"If thou seekest her as silver, and searchest for her as for hid treasures; Then shalt thou understand the fear of the Lord, and find the knowledge of God. For the Lord giveth wisdom: out of his mouth cometh knowledge and understanding"* Proverbs 2:4-6.

4.   Read: Proverbs 19:3 and Proverbs 8:11. What are the differences?

_____

_____

Repeat this prayer out loud:

Father, thank You for giving me, today, another day to prove myself as a real man according to Your principles. I put away foolish, earthly wisdom, and I accept responsibility for my actions in order to mature in Christ. Please help me find true wisdom, and give me the strategy I need for victory. Amen.

For Further Study

God gives wisdom for strategy – Proverbs 3:19; *"Blessed be the Lord my strength, which teacheth my hands to war, and my fingers to fight"* Psalm 144:1; *"Wisdom strengtheneth the wise more than ten mighty men which are in the city"* Ecclesiastes 7:19; Psalms 17:4; 44:5; 2 Corinthians 2:14; James 1:5.

Victory from strategy brings glory – *"Thine, O Lord, is the greatness, and the power, and the glory, and the victory, and the majesty"* 1 Chronicles 29:11; 2 Chronicles 20:12; *"Be not afraid nor dismayed by reason of this great multitude; for the battle is not your's, but God's ... Set yourselves, stand ye still, and see the salvation of the Lord with you ... fear not, nor be dismayed ... for the Lord will be with you"* 2 Chronicles 20:15-17; Glory – *"That, according as it is written, He that glorieth, let him glory in the Lord"* 1 Corinthians 1:31; *"But we all, with open face beholding as in a glass the glory of the Lord, are changed into the same image from glory to glory, even as by the Spirit of the Lord"* 2 Corinthians 3:18.

Self Test *Lesson 7*

1. How was Christ's greatness manifested and glorified?

    _____

2. Acceptance of _____ starts the maturation process in our lives.

3. When a child does something wrong, why is important for a parent to give him an opportunity to admit it?

    _____

4. Children may not always obey what you say, but they will always _____.

5. What was the major difference between King David and King Saul?

    _____

6. What is the difference between knowledge and wisdom?

    Knowledge is _____.

    Wisdom is _____.

7. What is the prerequisite for acquiring godly wisdom? *(circle one)*

    a. prayer   b. being an adult   c. fear of the Lord

8. When planning an event, it's wisdom to always consider the beginning before the ending.

    ___ True   ___ False

9. Use the words below to fill in the following sentence:

    wisdom   strategy   glory   victory

    To have _____, a _____ is needed; to obtain a _____, a

    _____ is required; to acquire _____, _____ is necessary.

10. Men who expect God to instantly change several years of living a careless and slack life can be guilty

    of what kind of thinking? _____

11. Where are strategies developed? _____

12. What is the lowest level of knowledge? _____

Lesson 8

Employed for Life &
Financial Freedom

Lesson 8
Employed for Life & Financial Freedom

I.   Employed for Life (Chapter 15)

    A.   Employment, both in the secular and sacred fields, creates _____ and

          _____. *(page 147)*

          1.   Unemployment creates a _____. *(page 147)*

          2.   Unemployment causes the loss of _____ in men. *(page 147)*

          3.   When a man cannot provide for himself or his own, he is robbed of his _____.
             (page 147)

    B.   Men were created in the image of God and given abilities and _____ and required to

          _____. What can happen when these abilities are stifled through unemployment?

          (page 147-148) _____

          _____

          _____

For Further Study

Employment basics – *"This we commanded you, that if any would not work, neither should he eat"*
2 Thessalonians 3:10; *"Wealth from gambling quickly disappears; wealth from hard work grows"* Proverbs 13:11
TLB; *"Work brings profit; talk brings poverty!"* Proverbs 14:23 TLB; *"Blessed is every one that feareth the Lord;
that walketh in his own ways. For thou shalt eat the labour of thine hands: happy shalt thou be, and it shall be
well with thee"* Psalm 128:1-2.

Adam created in God's image, given a job to steward the earth – Genesis 1:26-31; *"Thou madest him to have
dominion over the works of thy hands; thou hast put all things under his feet"* Psalm 8:6; The human reproductive
process satisfies – Genesis 1:28; *"As arrows are in the hand of a mighty man; so are children of the youth"*
Psalm 127:3-5.

C.   What is the main reason for the "work ethic"? *(page 148)* _____

D.   Define the expression, "welfare mentality." *(page 150)* _____
_____

E.   Who are "spiritually unemployed" Christians? *(pages 151)* _____
_____
_____

1.   Who does a "welfare mentality" Christian depend on for his wisdom? *(circle one)* *(page 150)*
     a.   the pastor   b.   the Lord   c.   his spouse

2.   What do the spiritually unemployed miss out on? *(circle one)* *(page 151-152)*
     a.   an opportunity to hear the "inside track"   b.   the excitement of serving Christ

3.   What is one of the greatest "highs" a man can experience? *(circle one)* *(page 152)*
     a.   praying for someone who starts a new relationship with Christ
     b.   making his first million dollars
     c.   praying for someone to make his first million dollars

For Further Study

Working for the Lord – *"If a man therefore purge himself from these, he shall be a vessel unto honour, sanctified, and meet for the master's use, and prepared unto every good work"* 2 Timothy 2:21; *"Therefore, my beloved brethren, be ye stedfast, unmoveable, always abounding in the work of the Lord, forasmuch as ye know that your labour is not in vain in the Lord"* 1 Corinthians 15:58; Exodus 35.

Reward workers – 1 Corinthians 9:7-10; Timothy 5:18; Ministers' wives who work alongside their husbands deserve compensation – Romans 15:27, 28 TLB; Proverbs 13:11, 12; *"For the workman deserves his support (his living, his food)"* – Matthew 10:10 AMP.

How to build great works – *"A good man out of the good treasure of his heart bringeth forth that which is good"* Luke 6:45; Hebrews 1:3; 11:3; Ephesians 4:29; *"Who is a wise man and endued with knowledge among you? let him show out of a good conversation his works with meekness of wisdom"* James 3:13.

F. How does a Christian discover his ministry gifts? *(pages 153)*

_____

_____

G. Name some ways of being spiritually employed. *(page 153)*

_____   _____

_____   _____

H. Read: *"Therefore, my beloved brethren, be ye stedfast, unmoveable, always abounding in the work of the Lord, forasmuch as ye know that your labour is not in vain in the Lord"* 1 Corinthians 15:58.

II. Financial Freedom (Chapter 16)

A. Waste is taking the best of what you have and using it on the _____, then giving what you have left to the _____. *(page 155)*

For Further Study

Reap where you sow spiritually – 1 Corinthians 9:11, 13-14.

Discover your gifts – *"But watch thou in all things, endure afflictions, do the work of an evangelist, make full proof of thy ministry"* 2 Timothy 4:5; *"Allow God's creativity to work in you"* Psalm 37:4.

Do Christ's works – *"He that believeth on me, the works that I do shall he do also; and greater works than these shall he do; because I go unto my Father"* John 14:12; Matthew 21:21; Mark 11:22-24.

Produce abundance – *"And God is able to make all grace abound toward you; that ye, always having all sufficiency in all things, may abound in every good work"* 2 Corinthians 9:8; *"The thief cometh not, but for to steal, and to kill, and to destroy: I am come that they might have life, and that they might have it more abundantly"* John 10:10.

1. By giving to God, we gain something that is _____
   _____. *(page 156)*

2. The _____ of _____ is often the "acid test" of a man's character. *(page 156)*

B. Read: Malachi 1:5-10.

C. Jesus didn't discourage riches, but name three deceits of riches He warned about. *(page 158)*

1. _____

2. _____

3. _____

D. How are non-tithers similar to non-voters? *(page 160)*

_____

E. What is the outcome of men tithing, giving gifts and making contributions? *(page 163)*

_____
_____
_____

For Further Study

Honoring God – *"A son honoureth his father, and a servant his master: if then I be a father, where is mine honour? and if I be a master, where is my fear? saith the Lord of hosts unto you, O priests, that despise my name. And ye say, Wherein have we despised thy name?"* Malachi 1:6; *"Will a man rob God? Yet ye have robbed me. But ye say, Wherein have we robbed thee? In tithes and offerings"* Malachi 3:8; *"And I will rebuke the devourer for your sakes, and he shall not destroy the fruits of your ground; neither shall your vine cast her fruit before the time in the field, saith the Lord of hosts"* Malachi 3:11; Luke 18:9-14.

Giving to God is never a waste – *"But when his disciples saw it, they had indignation, saying, To what purpose is this waste? For this ointment might have been sold for much, and given to the poor"* Matthew 26:8-9; John 12:4-6; *"For ye have the poor always with you; but me ye have not always"* Matthew 26:11.

F.   Fill in the blanks with the following words. *(page 163)*

faith   prayer   disobedience   limitations   sacrifice

1.   You cannot compensate through _____ what you lose through

_____.

2.   God puts no _____ on _____; and _____

puts no _____ on God.

Practical:

1.   Read: *"The thief cometh not, but for to steal, and to kill, and to destroy: I am come that they might have life, and that they might have it more abundantly"* John 10:10. In what ways has Satan worked against you in relation to your employment?

_____

_____

For Further Study

Giving basics – *"Give, and it shall be given unto you; good measure, pressed down, and shaken together, and running over, shall men give into your bosom. For with the same measure that ye mete withal it shall be measured to you again"* Luke 6:38; *"But godliness with contentment is great gain"* 1 Timothy 6:6; *"For where your treasure is, there will your heart be also"* Matthew 6:21; *"The first of the firstfruits of thy land thou shalt bring unto the house of the Lord thy God"* Exodus 34:26; *"Honour the Lord with thy substance, and with the firstfruits of all thine increase"* Proverbs 3:9; *"And all the tithe of the land, whether of the seed of the land, or of the fruit of the tree, is the Lord's: it is holy unto the Lord"* Leviticus 27:30; *"Offer unto God thanksgiving; and pay thy vows unto the most High: And call upon me in the day of trouble: I will deliver thee, and thou shalt glorify me"* Psalm 50:12-15; 2 Corinthians 8:1-5; Luke 19:5-9; Acts 10:2-8; 2 Corinthians 8.

2. "You gain by giving what you cannot buy with money." List a time when you saw this principle operate in your own life or in the life of someone you know. _____

_____

3. In your opinion, why would the use of money reveal a man's heart?

_____

_____

Repeat this prayer out loud:

Thank you, Lord, for this new understanding of how I can be fulfilled in my Christian walk. Help me find and fulfill all the gifts and talents I can offer You. And forgive me for not giving of my money and myself as I should have in times past. I commit to being a good tither and to give my time, as well, for Your Kingdom. Amen.

For Further Study

"You cannot compensate by sacrificial giving what you lose through disobedience – And on the morrow, when they were come from Bethany, he was hungry: And seeing a fig tree afar off having leaves, he came, if haply he might find any thing thereon: and when he came to it, he found nothing but leaves; for the time of figs was not yet. And Jesus answered and said unto it, No man eat fruit of thee hereafter for ever" Mark 11:12-14; *"And Samuel said, Hath the Lord as great delight in burnt offerings and sacrifices, as in obeying the voice of the Lord? Behold, to obey is better than sacrifice, and to hearken than the fat of rams"* 1 Samuel 15:22; *"He that hath my commandments, and keepeth them, he it is that loveth me: and he that loveth me shall be loved of my Father, and I will love him, and will manifest myself to him"* John 14:21; *"Verily I say unto you, Wheresoever this gospel shall be preached in the whole world, there shall also this, that this woman hath done, be told for a memorial of her"* Matthew 26:13.

Self Test *Lesson 8*

1. If a man cannot be productive, he will lack: *(circle all that apply)*

   a. dignity   b. creativity   c. self-esteem   d. fulfillment

2. What is often the effect of unemployment in men's lives? _____

   _____

   _____

3. Socialism in all its forms is a proven failure.   ___ True ___ False

4. Why is America today in danger of destruction? _____

   _____

   _____

5. Name three examples of being "spiritually employed."

   a. _____

   b. _____

   c. _____

6. Christians can discover their ministry gifts by serving others.   ___ True ___ False

7. Summarize what Malachi said about bringing polluted offerings to God. _____

   _____

   _____

8. Sometimes giving to God can be wasteful.   ___ True ___ False

9. What is often the "acid test" of character in a man? _____

10. A man reveals the condition of his heart by his _____ toward money.

11. Non-tithers and non-voters are similar because they are both _____.

12. It is possible to compensate for not tithing by coming to God in prayer and asking Him to bless the work of
    your hand regardless.   ___ True ___ False

Lesson 9

Positive Stress &
Peace for All Seasons

Lesson 9
Positive Stress & Peace for All Seasons

I. Positive Stress (Chapter 17)

    A. Pressure always _____. *(fill in the blank)* *(page 165)*

        overwhelms   magnifies   tests

        1. Name five temptations Elijah faced. *(page 166)*

            a. _____   d. _____

            b. _____   e. _____

            c. _____

        2. Stress is _____ to life. *(page 166)*

    B. Indicate whether the following statements are True or False. *(pages 167-168)*

        1. Television is a great way to reduce stress.   ___ True ___ False

        2. Personal debt on the individual level kills productivity.   ___ True ___ False

        3. Young married couples can be seduced to try to accumulate in three years of marriage what took their parents thirty years to obtain.   ___ True ___ False

---

For Further Study

"Then answered Jesus and said unto them, Verily, verily, I say unto you, The Son can do nothing of himself, but what he seeth the Father do: for what things soever he doeth, these also doeth the Son likewise. For the Father loveth the Son, and sheweth him all things that himself doeth: and he will shew him greater works than these, that ye may marvel" John 5:19-20.

"Verily, verily, I say unto you, He that believeth on me, the works that I do shall he do also; and greater works than these shall he do; because I go unto my Father" John 14:12; *"If I do not the works of my Father, believe me not. But if I do, though ye believe not me, believe the works: that ye may know, and believe, that the Father is in me, and I in him"* John 10:37-38.

"For he taught them as one having authority, and not as the scribes" Matthew 7:29.

C. Financial pressure, like any stress, can drive men to _____ but needn't _____ the real man. *(page 168)*

D. Read: *"You are a poor specimen if you can't stand the pressure of adversity"* Proverbs 24:10 TLB.

E. Pressure is normal and even needed in life. The right amount of tension in a guitar or piano is necessary for _____. *(page 169)*

  1. The more pressure matter is able to withstand, the more _____ it becomes. It's the same with _____. *(page 169)*

  2. The greater the responsibility, the greater the _____. *(page 170)*

F. What was the phrase that changed Joseph's life when under pressure? *(circle one)* *(page 170)*

  "But God"   "Be Happy"   "Believe in Yourself"   "It's Your Right"

  1. All trials and temptations will end positively if: *(circle one)* *(page 170)*
      a. you just hang in there   b. you commit it to God   c. you pray long enough

  2. It is the _____ of _____ to change things in our lives for good. *(page 170)*

For Further Study

Rejoice, even in trials – *"My brethren, count it all joy when ye fall into divers temptations; Knowing this, that the trying of your faith worketh patience. But let patience have her perfect work, that ye may be perfect and entire, wanting nothing"* James 1:2-4; Genesis 50:20; Romans 5:3-5; 1 Peter 1:6-7; 4:12-13.

Reward for overcomers – "the crown of life" James 1:12; "my new name" Revelation 3:12

"Be careful for nothing; but in every thing by prayer and supplication with thanksgiving let your requests be made known unto God" Philippians 4:6; *"Whom resist stedfast in the faith, knowing that the same afflictions are accomplished in your brethren that are in the world"* 1 Peter 5:9.

"Who shall separate us from the love of Christ? shall tribulation, or distress, or persecution, or famine, or nakedness, or peril, or sword? ... Nay, in all these things we are more than conquerors through him that loved" Romans 8:35-37.

G. List some of the positive aspects of stress. *(page 169)*

1. _____

2. _____

3. _____

4. _____

5. _____

II. Peace for All Seasons (Chapter 18)

A. Peace comes from _____. *(page 172)*

    1. According to the Bible, peace does not come through treaties, summit conferences or negotiated settlements as long as men have _____ in their _____. *(page 173)*

    2. Little or no peace comes from: *(circle one)* *(page 174)*
       a. negotiated compromise   b. a total victory   c. prayer

B. Read: *"The words of his mouth were smoother than butter, But war was in his heart; His words were softer than oil, Yet they were drawn swords"* Psalm 55:21 NKJV.

For Further Study

"Draw me not away with the wicked, and with the workers of iniquity, which speak peace to their neighbours, but mischief is in their hearts" Psalm 28:3.

  "Glory to God … peace among men with whom He is well-pleased – men of good will, of His favor" Luke 2:14 AMP. Find the peace of God – Psalms 22:5; 28:7; 85:8; Isaiah 12:2; 26:3; John 14:27; 16:33; *"And let the peace of God rule in your hearts, to the which also ye are called in one body; and be ye thankful"* Colossians 3:15; *"Now the Lord of peace himself give you peace always by all means"* 2 Thessalonians 3:16; *"The Lord bless thee, and keep thee: … make his face shine upon thee … be gracious unto thee; … lift up his countenance upon thee, and give thee peace"* Numbers 6:24-26.

"Seek peace, and pursue it" Psalm 34:14; 1 Peter 3:11; *"Better a dry morsel, and quietness therewith, than a house full of sacrifices with strife"* Proverbs 17:1

C. Name three major requirements for victory. *(page 175)*

    1. _____

    2. _____

    3. _____

D. Jesus refused to receive reward without paying the price because He knew the principle of

    "No _____, no _____." *(page 175)*

    1. Why can Jesus offer mankind total peace? *(page 175)* _____

    _____

    2. The peace that this world offers is _____, _____ and

    without _____ substance. *(page 175)*

    3. Read: *"Peace I leave with you, My peace I give to you; not as the world gives do I give to you. Let not your heart be troubled, neither let it be afraid"* John 14:27 NKJV.

E. Fill in the blanks to complete the following statements: *(page 176)*

    1. Men who live by _____ are strong.

    Men who live by _____ are weak.

    2. To the degree men yield to temptations, there is a loss of both _____ and _____. *(page 176)*

For Further Study

Jesus' wilderness temptation – Luke 4

"Peace I leave with you, my peace I give unto you: not as the world giveth, give I unto you. Let not your heart be troubled, neither let it be afraid" John 14:27.

"For the flesh lusteth against the Spirit, and the Spirit against the flesh: and these are contrary the one to the other: so that ye cannot do the things that ye would" Galatians 5:17.

"From whence come wars and fightings among you? come they not hence, even of your lusts that war in your members" James 4:1.

"For to be carnally minded is death; but to be spiritually minded is life and peace" Romans 8:6.

F.   Write the correct letter next to the phrase to complete each principle. *(pages 176-178)*

_____ What is yielded to grows	a.	power
_____ What is resisted grows	b.	godly
_____ You cannot overcome sin with	c.	easier
_____ Fighting for victory is	d.	difficult
_____ Fighting is _____ than bearing consequences.	e.	a truce
_____ The place of agreement is the place of	f.	weaker
_____ Submitting to what is _____ produces resistance to sin.	g.	stronger

G.   Read: *"A righteous man who falters before the wicked is like a murky spring and a polluted well"* Proverbs 25:26 NKJV.

1.   What was Joshua's mistake in dealing with the Gibeonites? *(page 177)*

_____

2.   Everything in life is under our _____ of _____. *(page 179)*

3.   Once we make a choice, we become a _____ to that choice. *(page 179)*

H.   Men often lose their peace by opening their _____ when they should keep them

_____. *(page 180)*

For Further Study

"A righteous man falling down before the wicked is as a troubled fountain, and a corrupt spring" Proverbs 25:26.
 "Know ye not, that to whom ye yield yourselves servants to obey, his servants ye are to whom ye obey; whether of sin unto death, or of obedience unto righteousness" Romans 6:16.
"But he, knowing their thoughts, said unto them, Every kingdom divided against itself is brought to desolation; and a house divided against a house falleth" Luke 11:17; Matthew 18:8-9.
God's way – *"Teach me thy way, O Lord; I will walk in thy truth: unite my heart to fear thy name"* Psalm 86:11; *"For my yoke is easy, and my burden is light"* Matthew 11:30; *"Let us therefore follow after the things which make for peace, and things wherewith one may edify another"* Romans 14:19.
"All things are lawful unto me, but all things are not expedient: all things are lawful for me, but I will not be brought under the power of any" 1 Corinthians 6:12.

Practical:

1. Name a positive aspect of stress. *(page 169)* _____

2. In your opinion, what is the spiritual significance of the difference between a "soldier's war" and a "politician's war"? *(page 174-175)*

    _____

    _____

3. Read: John 14:27. How can Jesus make this claim when we're under so much pressure on earth?

    _____

    _____

4. When all is said and done, what is the best way to achieve peace in your life?

    _____

    _____

Repeat this prayer out loud:

Father, I have faced temptations and often given in, and for that, I repent. I have also lost my peace instead of learning to maintain it. Thank You that this is now covered by Christ's blood. I trust You to guide me as I commit to overcome Satan's work in my life. In Jesus' Name, I pray, Amen.

For Further Study

"There remaineth therefore a rest to the people of God" Hebrews 4:9; *"And the peace of God, which passeth all understanding, shall keep your hearts and minds through Christ Jesus"* Philippians 4:7.
"Great peace have they which love thy law: and nothing shall offend them" Psalm 119:165.
"For God is not the author of confusion, but of peace, as in all churches of the saints" 1 Corinthians 14:33.
"For unto us a child is born, unto us a son is given ... and his name shall be called Wonderful, Counsellor, The mighty God, The everlasting Father, The Prince of Peace" Isaiah 9:6
"He is our peace, who hath ... broken down the middle wall of partition between us ... so making peace; ... that he might reconcile both unto God in one body by the cross ... and preached peace" Ephesians 2:14-17.
"Exclaiming, Would that you had known personally ... the things that make for peace (for freedom from all the distresses that are experienced as the result of sin and upon which your peace, that is, your security, safety, prosperity and happiness depends)" Luke 19:42 AMP.

Self Test *Lesson 9*

1. There is no such thing as good or positive stress. ___ True ___ False

2. What's the difference between carbon, graphite and diamonds? _____

3. The more _____ matter is able to withstand, the more valuable it becomes.

4. Name some positive aspects of stress.

    a. _____

    b. _____

    c. _____

    d. _____

5. How can trials and temptations have a positive end?

    _____

6. God always starts on a _____ and ends on a _____.

7. Where does absolute peace actually come from in our lives? _____

8. God demanded that His people often make treaties with their enemies. ___ True ___ False

9. Lust is an enemy God wants us to negotiate a truce with. ___ True ___ False

10. Men can set at a peace table and sign a peace treaty yet still have war in their _____.

11. Men who live by conviction are _____; men who live by convenience are _____.

12. What was a major truth Jesus knew that kept Him from compromising with Satan?

    _____

    _____

13. Submission to the godly will bring resistance to the devilish and _____ over the _____.

14. Everything in life is under the power of choice. Once the choice is made, you become _____

    _____.

Lesson 10
Leadership That Works

Lesson 10
Leadership That Works

A. Leadership _____ are inherent in the nature of every man. *(page 181)*

   1. Three distinguishing characteristics of popular leaders who command a following are: *(page 181)*

      a. _____

      b. _____

      c. _____

   2. All three of these found in one man can change the _____. *(page 181)*

For Further Study

Jesus' testimony – *"I and my Father are one"* John 10:30. *"I can of mine own self do nothing: as I hear, I judge: and my judgment is just; because I seek not mine own will, but the will of the Father which hath sent me"* John 5:30; *"For I came down from heaven, not to do mine own will, but the will of him that sent me"* John 6:38. *"And they come to Jerusalem: and Jesus went into the temple, and began to cast out them that sold and bought in the temple, and overthrew the tables of the moneychangers, and the seats of them that sold doves; And would not suffer that any man should carry any vessel through the temple. And he taught, saying unto them, Is it not written, My house shall be called of all nations the house of prayer? but ye have made it a den of thieves"* Mark 11:15-17.
Qualifications for leadership – 1 Timothy 3
Inconsistency is immaturity and hinders those around us – Proverbs 25:19; James 1:8, 4:8.

B. 1 Timothy 3:2-7 gives six major qualifications for true leadership. List each of the qualities found in the Scripture under its appropriate category of the qualifications for leadership. *(pages 182-188)*

Reputation	Ethics	Morality
_____	_____	_____
_____	_____	_____
_____	_____	_____
_____	_____	_____

Temperament	Habits	Maturity
_____	_____	_____
_____	_____	_____
_____	_____	_____
_____	_____	_____

For Further Study

Maturity from accepting responsibility – Acts 13:22; Immaturity from refusal to accept responsibility – Proverbs 16:2, 21:2; Genesis 3:11-12.

We alone are responsible for our lives – 2 Corinthians 5:10.

Every man is accountable for six areas of responsibility – Reputation – 1 Thessalonians 5:22, 2 Corinthians 6:3; Ethics – 1 Timothy 4:16; Morality and Temperament – 2 Timothy 2:24, 25; Habits – 1 Timothy 4:8; Maturity – 1 Timothy 4:15.

Maturation is a lifelong process – *"You, therefore, must be perfect [growing into complete maturity of godliness in mind and character, having reached the proper height of virtue and integrity], as your heavenly Father is perfect"* Matthew 5:48 AMP; Romans 5:3-5, 8:37; Galatians 6:9; Hebrews 3:6, 6:1; 1 John 3:2, 3.

C. A man's reputation is seen in the regard given his _____. *(page 182)*

D. A real man will value his reputation with his _____ more than the regard he has with his peers. *(page 183)*

    1. Ethical behavior by parents in regard to children is necessary to _____ relationships. *(page 183)*

    2. Where _____ are missing, there is no foundation for ethical behavior. *(page 184)*

    3. Immoral or religious ethics are represented in the New Testament by the _____ and _____. *(page 184)*

E. Morality is a system of _____ conduct. Morality can be called _____, which can, in one sense, be used in the Bible synonymously with _____. *(page 184)*

    1. Moral cowardice is the _____; moral courage is its virtue. *(page 184)*

    2. Men often fail to qualify for leadership because of _____. *(page 185)*

For Further Study

A good reputation – *"A good name is rather to be chosen than great riches, and loving favour rather than silver and gold"* Proverbs 22:1; *"A good name is better than precious ointment"* Ecclesiastes 7:1.

A bad reputation – *"The memory of the just is blessed: but the name of the wicked shall rot"* Proverbs 10:7; *"Thou hast rebuked the heathen, thou hast destroyed the wicked, thou hast put out their name for ever and ever"* Psalm 9:5.

A good name – *"Whoever heard me spoke well of me"* Job 29:11 NIV (also vs. 7-17).

A bad name – *"that wicked man Nabal. He is just like his name — his name is Fool"* 1 Samuel 25 NIV.

A man's name is only as good as his word – *"A good man is known by his truthfulness; a false man by deceit and lies"* Proverbs 12:17 TLB.

Choose character – Proverbs 31:23, 30, 31.

F. List six reasons men need courage. *(page 185)*

1. _____   4. _____

2. _____   5. _____

3. _____   6. _____

G. A temperate man doesn't make decisions based on _____
_____
_____. *(page 186-187)*

The real man's criteria for decision-making are: *(page 187)*

_____

For Further Study

The double-minded waiver between right and wrong – 1 Kings 18:21; They profess to hate sin but have a lingering love for it – James 4:1; They do not have a right understanding of good and evil – Hebrews 5:14.

Character is built in private, developed out of a lifetime of individual decisions which either enhance or diminish it – *"I have chosen the way of truth: thy judgments have I laid before me"* Psalm 119:30; *"If a man therefore purge himself from these, he shall be a vessel unto honour, sanctified, and meet for the master's use, and prepared unto every good work"* 2 Timothy 2:21.

It takes courage to make decisions – *"Choose you this day whom ye will serve ... but as for me and my house, we will serve the Lord"* Joshua 24:15.

Decision translates into energy – 2 Chronicles 2:1; Habakkuk 2:2; *"A double minded man is unstable in all his ways"* James 1:8.

H. Physical habits find their root in _____. *(page 187)*

    1. What did "high places" represent in the Old Testament? *(page 187)* _____

        _____

    2. Give some examples of "high places" in men's minds today. *(page 187)* _____

        _____

    3. Habits can be developed by _____ or _____. *(page 188)*

I. The marks of a mature man can be seen in various ways. Name some of them. *(page 188)*

    _____

    _____

    1. Leaders are men who _____ to influence. *(page 188)*

    2. Followers only _____ to influence. *(page 188)*

J. Today, God is looking for men to accept the spiritual and _____ leadership of the

    _____, _____ and _____. *(page 190)*

For Further Study

High places – *"And also concerning Maachah the mother of Asa the king, he removed her from being queen, because she had made an idol in a grove: and Asa cut down her idol, and stamped it, and burnt it at the brook Kidron. But the high places were not taken away out of Israel: nevertheless the heart of Asa was perfect all his days"* 2 Chronicles 15:16-17.

"That he might sanctify and cleanse it with the washing of water by the word" Ephesians 5:26.

"For if thou altogether holdest thy peace at this time, then shall there enlargement and deliverance arise to the Jews from another place; but thou and thy father's house shall be destroyed: and who knoweth whether thou art come to the kingdom for such a time as this?" Esther 4:14.

"For the vision is yet for an appointed time, but at the end it shall speak, and not lie: though it tarry, wait for it; because it will surely come, it will not tarry" Habakkuk 2:3.

K. The first and foremost thing a real man does is establish his _____ to God. *(page 190)*

Practical:

1. Read: Proverbs 22:1. What do people associate with your name? *(not necessary to write it down)*

2. Think about "high places" and the fact that habits stem from mental traits. What habits do you need to change? Can you determine to change them, or will they happen by default?

    _____

    _____

    _____

3. Discuss with someone what it means to you personally that today is a day for "Daniels."

Repeat this prayer out loud:

Father, I accept my God-given responsibility as a man to be a leader. I know some of my failures, and I'm sure there are many more that I am not even aware of. I repent for all my sin, both known and unknown, and ask for Your wisdom, Your guidance to help me start to excel in leading. I trust You for it. Amen.

For Further Study

Lay a right foundation for your character – 2 Corinthians 7:1.
"I have refrained my feet from every evil way, that I might keep thy word. I have not departed from thy judgments: for thou hast taught me ... Through thy precepts I get understanding: therefore I hate every false way" Psalm 119:101, 102, 104.
If you make a quality decision to honor God in your thoughts, words, motives and deeds, God will honor you –
"If any man serve me, let him follow me; and where I am, there shall also my servant be: if any man serve me, him will my Father honour" John 12:26.

Self Test *Lesson 10*

1. Men are born with an _____.

2. Name three characteristics in popular leaders.

   a. _____

   b. _____

   c. _____

3. "Fervent in spirit" is likened unto what? _____

   _____

4. Identifying with purposes and goals in life without thought to self is a good definition of what?

   _____

5. Because of a man's need to provide for his family, his reputation within his workplace is by far more important than his reputation at home. ___ True ___ False

6. A lack of ethics can blind a man to his own: *(circle one)*

   a. good fortune   b. wrong doing   c. happiness

7. Immoral but religious ethics are represented in the New Testament by whom?

   _____

8. What is a major reason many men fail to qualify for leadership? _____

9. Retired Secretary of the Navy, James H. Webb, Jr. said, "Courage, both moral and physical, is a character trait that can _____."

10. A man's criteria for decision-making should be what?

    a. _____   c. _____

    b. _____   d. _____

11. In Old Testament times, the continued allowance of "high places" led to the official reinstitution of:

    a. paganism   b. witchcraft   c. idolatry

12. Habits can be developed by default or _____.

    Change a mind, change a _____, change a life.

The Irresistible Husband &
The Fabulous Father

Lesson 11
The Irresistible Husband & The Fabulous Father

I.   The Irresistible Husband (Chapter 20)

    A.   Correcting problems in marriage must be handled with _____ and understanding. *(page 192)*

        1.   While sin desensitizes emotions and concerns for others, the _____ brings sensitivity to other's needs, hurts and desires. *(page 192)*

        2.   The very nature of God is to work _____. *(page 193)*

        3.   How do the characteristics of a gentleman display themselves? *(page 193)*

            _____

            _____

For Further Study

A man of God gives his word in marriage and keeps it, no matter how difficult – *"Therefore guard your passions! Keep faith with the wife of your youth. For the Lord, the God of Israel, says he hates divorce and cruel men. Therefore control your passions – let there be no divorcing of your wives"* Malachi 2:15-16 TLB.

The family of a man of God can depend on him – *"A faithful man shall abound with blessings"* Proverbs 28:20.

 "Now the works of the flesh are manifest, which are these; Adultery, fornication, uncleanness, lasciviousness, Idolatry, witchcraft, hatred, variance, emulations, wrath, strife, seditions, heresies, Envyings, murders, drunkenness, revellings, and such like: of the which I tell you before, as I have also told you in time past, that they which do such things shall not inherit the kingdom of God" Galatians 5:19-21.

B.   Which Scripture mentioned is a "biblical bidding" for courtesy? *(page 194)* _____

_____

1.   Read: *"But the fruit of the Spirit is love, joy, peace, longsuffering, gentleness, goodness, faith, Meekness, temperance: against such there is no law. And they that are Christ's have crucified the flesh with the affections and lusts"* Galatians 5:22-24.

2.   What is the "fruit" of the Spirit to be in a man's life as listed on *pages 194-195?*

_____

C.   Lessons learned from aspects of the "fruit":

1.   When a man knows his strength, he can afford to be _____. *(page 194)*

2.   Women were created to _____ men. *(page 194)*

3.   Recognition of others' _____ demonstrates strength. *(page 195)*

4.   When a man satisfies a woman's uniqueness, she will become _____

_____. *(page 196)*

For Further Study

"Do nothing out of selfish ambition or vain conceit, but in humility consider others better than yourselves" Philippians 2:3 NIV.

"Thou hast also given me the shield of thy salvation: and thy gentleness hath made me great" 2 Samuel 22:36.

"Be kindly affectioned one to another with brotherly love; in honour preferring one another" Romans 12:10.

"With all lowliness and meekness, with longsuffering, forbearing one another in love" Ephesians 4:2.

"Put on therefore, as the elect of God, holy and beloved, bowels of mercies, kindness, humbleness of mind, meekness, longsuffering" Colossians 3:12.

"Now the man Moses was very meek, above all the men which were upon the face of the earth" Numbers 12:3.

D. Marriage is the _____ most important relationship men and women will ever have, and the choice of a mate is the second most important _____ they will ever make. *(page 198)*

II. The Fabulous Father (Chapter 21)

A. The legacy of fathers is in their _____. *(page 199)*

    1. As a father, a man should serve his family as Christ served the church, as: *(page 199)*

        a. _____   b. _____   c. _____

    2. What are the responsibilities of each role? *(page 199)*

        a. _____

        b. _____

        c. _____

          _____

For Further Study

The marriage covenant – *"Yet she is thy companion and the wife of thy covenant"* Malachi 2:14; *"A man should give his wife all that is her right as a married woman; and the wife should do the same for the husband"* 1 Corinthians 7:3 TLB; *"Keep faith with the wife of your youth"* Malachi 2:15 TLB; *"Honor your marriage and its vows and be pure; for God will surely punish all those who are immoral or commit adultery"* Hebrews 13:4 TLB.
Love, not lust – John 10:10; 15:13; 1 Corinthians 13:5; Ephesians 5:25; 2 Timothy 3:2; Hebrews 13:4; James 4:1-3.
Teach and train – *"Impress them on your children"* – Deuteronomy 6:5-9 NIV; *"Teach them to your children"* Deuteronomy 11:18-21 NIV; Ephesians 6:4; Colossians 3:16; 1 Thessalonians 4:1-8.
What to teach – *"Set an example … in speech, in life, in love, in faith and in purity"* 1 Timothy 4:11-13 NIV; Titus 2:2-8.
Father's responsibilities for children – Ephesians 6:4; Colossians 3:21; 1 Timothy 3:4, 12

B. Give a definition of "solipsism." *(page 199)* _____

C. How has this changed our young people in regard to satisfaction? *(page 199)*

_____

_____

_____

D. What were the comparative figures given regarding students' time spent watching television versus receiving education? *(page 200)*

_____

_____

E. What is the "greatest mission" for men today? *(page 201)* _____

_____

For Further Study

Live within your means – *"Stay away from the love of money; be satisfied with what you have. For God has said, 'I will never, never fail you nor forsake you'"* Hebrews 13:5 TLB; *"But godliness with contentment is great gain"* 1 Timothy 6:6.

Produce, don't just consume – *"A man shall be satisfied with good by the fruit of his mouth: and the recompence of a man's hands shall be rendered unto him"* Proverbs 12:14; *"Lazy people want much but get little, while the diligent are prospering"* Proverbs 13:4 TLB; *"Steady plodding brings prosperity; hasty speculation brings poverty"* Proverbs 21:5 TLB.

"I have no greater joy than to hear that my children walk in truth" 3 John 4.

1. These principles for life are first and foremost to be taught where? *(page 202)* _____

   _____

2. Young men must be _____ in the ways of morality, goodness and righteousness.

   This is the responsibility of _____ men who have found the answers through Christ. *(page 202)*

3. Read: *"You younger men, follow the leadership of those who are older"* 1 Peter 5:5 TLB.

4. Men are _____, not owners of their children. *(page 204)*

5. Good fathering doesn't happen by chance, but takes _____, _____

   and _____. *(page 205)*

6. Children may not always listen to you, but they will always _____ you. *(page 206)*

For Further Study

David's example – *"Now his father, King David, had never disciplined him [Adonijah] at any time—not so much as by a single scolding! He was a very handsome man, and was Absalom's younger brother"* 1 Kings 1:6 TLB.
Abraham's example – *"He will direct his children and his household after him to keep the way of the Lord by doing what is right and just"* Genesis 18:19 NIV.
Good fathering includes discipline – *"Even a child is known by his doings, whether his work be pure, and whether it be right"* Proverbs 20:11; *"Train up a child in the way he should go: and when he is old, he will not depart from it … Foolishness is bound in the heart of a child; but the rod of correction shall drive it far from him"* Proverbs 22:6, 15; *"Withhold not correction from the child: for if thou beatest him with the rod, he shall not die"* Proverbs 23:13; *"And, ye fathers, provoke not your children to wrath: but bring them up in the nurture and admonition of the Lord"* Ephesians 6:4.

Practical:

1. Write out Philippians 2:3. _____

_____

2. Read: 1 Peter 5:5. What is your responsibility to the next generation?

_____

3. What is meant by the phrase, "It is not the father's responsibility to make all his children's decisions for them but to let them see him make his." *(page 206)*

_____

Repeat this prayer out loud:

Father, in so many ways, I've done wrong for my own children and for the young people of the next generation. I acknowledge my errors, repent today and ask You, Lord, to help me do right from now on. Please make me, in both word and deed, an example of true manhood and a leader of the young. Amen.

For Further Study

Who should teach – Fathers and mothers – Proverbs 1:8, 9; 4:1; 6:20-24; Elders – 1 Timothy 1:18; 4:14
Fathers have a God-given responsibility to their offspring. Fathers are blessed when they raise their children in the fear and admonition of the Lord – Deuteronomy 11:18-21. Fathers are cursed if they neglect their family responsibility – Proverbs 17:25.
Job's example – Job 29:4-25

Self Test *Lesson 11*

1. Some of the characteristics of a gentleman are displayed in:

   a. _____   c. _____

   b. _____   d. _____

2. What is the opposite of a "Fabulous Father"? _____

3. Christ fulfilled three major roles; a father is to do the same. What are they?

   a. _____   b. _____   c. _____

4. In a recent survey, for every seven hours spent watching television, how many hours did children spend

   reading? _____

5. The greatest mission for men today is not to correct what is wrong in adults, but:

   _____

6. Another survey listed four basic causes why children become vulnerable and susceptible to drugs and

   alcohol. What are they?

   a. _____   c. _____

   b. _____   d. _____

7. A father's responsibility in the home is to provide intimacy, _____, _____ and

   _____.

8. Men can pass on to children only what they possess themselves.   ___ True   ___ False

9. What is the "quickest way to destroy a child"? _____

10. Fathers are to guard against _____.

11. Godly fathers need to love as God loves: _____, _____

    and _____.

12. Children learn by example. It is not the father's responsibility to make all children's decisions for them but to

    _____.

Lesson 12

The Authentic Friend &
The Greatest Pleasure in Life

Lesson 12
The Authentic Friend & The Greatest Pleasure in Life

I.   The Authentic Friend (Chapter 22)

    A.   Faithful friends are life's _____. Being a true friend is one of

        the marks of a _____. *(page 209)*

        We learn how to be friends by studying the friendship of Jesus. *(page 211)*   ___ True   ___ False

        Read: John 15:13, 15; Proverbs 17:17; Proverbs 27:6.

    B.   Friends help in times of crisis, and the crisis _____ the relationship. *(page 211)*

    C.   True friends _____ when their friends do well. *(page 212)*

    D.   A wife who is a real friend to her husband is a man's greatest _____, _____

        of inspiration and _____. *(page 212)*

        1.   It is _____, not _____, that holds a marriage together. *(page 212)*

        2.   To make a friend, you must first be _____. *(page 212)*

For Further Study
Scriptures about friendships – 2 Samuel 13; 15:30-37; 16; 17
"A man of too many friends comes to ruin, But there is a friend who sticks closer than a brother" Proverbs 18:24.
"Then his wife said to him, 'Do you still hold fast your integrity? Curse God and die!'" Job 2:9.
"I am distressed for thee, my brother Jonathan: very pleasant hast thou been unto me: thy love to me was wonderful, passing the love of women" 2 Samuel 1:26.
"And the Scripture was fulfilled which says, 'And Abraham believed God, and it was reckoned to him as righteousness,' and he was called the friend of God" James 2:23.
"Thus the Lord used to speak to Moses face to face, just as a man speaks to his friend. When Moses returned to the camp, his servant Joshua, the son of Nun, a young man, would not depart from the tent" Exodus 33:11.

II. The Greatest Pleasure in Life (Chapter 23)

    A. God enjoys us. If we accept and understand that God takes pleasure in us succeeding, we will approach

        life _____, expecting to please Him and freely expressing the joy it brings. *(page 214)*

    B. The Bible counsels us to "have a walk worthy of the Lord, fully _____ Him." *(page 216)*

        1. Read: Colossians 1:10.

        2. Write out Philippians 2:13.

                _____

                _____

        3. Write out Revelations 4:12.

                _____

                _____

    C. To walk in God's will for our lives, as real men, _____ in our manhood and our

        _____ with Him, is our highest good. *(page 216)*

For Further Study

God's good pleasure – *"Having predestinated us unto the adoption of children by Jesus Christ to himself, according to the good pleasure of his will"* Ephesians 1:5; Ephesians 1:5-11; *"Wherefore also we pray always for you, that our God would count you worthy of this calling, and fulfil all the good pleasure of his goodness, and the work of faith with power"* 2 Thessalonians 1:11.
"For it pleased the Father that in him should all fulness dwell" Colossians 1:19.
"For as many as are led by the Spirit of God, they are the sons of God" Romans 8:14.

D. God has no pleasure in _____, nor the death of the _____. *(page 216)*

E. Our highest good gives God _____. *(page 216)*

F. God was not just pleased with Jesus as deity, but God was pleased in the very _____ that Jesus Christ displayed. We, too, can give God pleasure when we: *(page 216)*

1. _____

2. _____

3. _____

4. _____

5. _____

6. _____

G. Even when we sin and bring guilt and condemnation in our life, it is still possible to please God by our _____. *(page 217)*

For Further Study

What pleases God – *"Fear not, little flock; for it is your Father's good pleasure to give you the kingdom"* Luke 12:32.
"Have I any pleasure at all that the wicked should die? saith the Lord God: and not that he should return from his ways, and live?" Ezekiel 18:23.
"So then they that are in the flesh cannot please God" Romans 8:8.
"But without faith it is impossible to please him: for he that cometh to God must believe that he is, and that he is a rewarder of them that diligently seek him" Hebrews 11:6.
"And he that sent me is with me: the Father hath not left me alone; for I do always those things that please him" John 8:29.
"And lo a voice from heaven, saying, This is my beloved Son, in whom I am well pleased" Matthew 3:17.

Practical:

1. Read and comment on Proverbs 18:24. _____

    _____

2. What is better for a businessman than a customer? Why is this so important? *(page 212)*

    _____

    _____

3. Read: Psalm 5:4 and Ezekiel 33:11. Contrast these to what you know pleases God.

    _____

    _____

Repeat this prayer out loud:

Father, in Jesus' Name, I am a man. I want to be a real man. So those things in my life that are wrong, where I have made mistakes, committed errors and sins, forgive me. I want them out of my life. Right now, I ask You to come into my life by Your Spirit and change me. Make me to be the man You created me to be through Jesus Christ. Thank You, Lord. Amen.

For Further Study

"And whatsoever we ask, we receive of him, because we keep his commandments, and do those things that are pleasing in his sight" 1 John 3:22.

"Then shalt thou be pleased with the sacrifices of righteousness, with burnt offering and whole burnt offering: then shall they offer bullocks upon thine altar" Psalm 51:19; Psalm 69:30-31.

"If any man serve me, let him follow me; and where I am, there shall also my servant be: if any man serve me, him will my Father honour" John 12:26.

"Every man according as he purposeth in his heart, so let him give; not grudgingly, or of necessity: for God loveth a cheerful giver" 2 Corinthians 9:7.

"For the Lord taketh pleasure in his people: he will beautify the meek with salvation" Psalm 149:4.

"For after that in the wisdom of God the world by wisdom knew not God, it pleased God by the foolishness of preaching to save them that believe" 1 Corinthians 1:21.

Self Test *Lesson 12*

1. What can be life's greatest treasure? _____

2. What are some characteristics of "non-friends"?

    _____

3. What do times of crisis do to a true friendship? _____

4. What person can provide man with his greatest protection, source of inspiration and solace?

    _____

5. Romance is the most important component of a successful marriage. ___ True ___ False

6. How do you make a friend?

    _____

7. It is far more important for businessmen to concentrate on locating new customers than on developing

    more friendships. ___ True ___ False

8. As God is divine, it is irrelevant for us to consider that we can bring Him pleasure. ___ True ___ False

9. Living to our highest good produces what? _____

10. What are some ways we can give God pleasure according to Scripture?

    a. _____   d. _____

    b. _____   e. _____

    c. _____   f. _____

11. Is it possible to still please God when we've sinned? If so, how?

    _____

12. I want to be a real man. ___ True ___ False

Final Exam

1. The cheaper the merchandise, the _____.

2. Name the three things that limit every man in life.

   a. _____

   b. _____

   c. _____

3. _____ determines public performance.

4. What is the only thing left after the charm wears off? _____

5. Fame can come in a moment, but greatness comes with _____. *(fill in the blank)*

   longevity   pain   a price tag

6. A man's true integrity is found in: *(circle one)*

   a. his company worth   b. his ideal of himself   c. his personal character

7. The most powerful thing a man can do is create an image.   ___ True ___ False

8. Jesus taught that a man is only qualified to lead to the degree that he is _____.

9. Draw a line between phrases to create four basic principles.

   a. Communication is the   1. key to life.

   b. Exchange is the   2. power of life.

   c. Balance is the   3. process of life.

   d. Agreement is the   4. basis of life.

10. The only constant in maturity is _____.

11. Dying physically is the only form of death.   ___ True ___ False

12.   What must any "death" in Christ be followed by? _____

13.   Failing is the worst thing in the world that can happen to a man.   ___ True ___ False

14.   What is the essential ingredient in success? _____

15.   Man has been given what three basic responsibilities?

      a. _____   b. _____   c. _____

16.   The Kingdom of God runs on sentiment.   ___ True ___ False

17.   What is the least a real man must do who has the power to vote? *(circle one)*

      a. vote   b. help back candidates   c. go into politics

18.   From memory, name four ways God speaks to men.

      a. _____   c. _____

      b. _____   d. _____

19.   Name the six major steps of the Pattern of Revelation.

      a. _____   d. _____

      b. _____   e. _____

      c. _____   f. _____

20.   We are to find men who are extremely able and give them responsibility.   ___ True ___ False

21.   To qualify for our own, we must be faithful in that which is _____.

22.   What is a common type of treason in homes, businesses and churches? _____

23.   Trust can be extended without truth.   ___ True ___ False

24.   Place the following in their correct order of priority.

      Wife   God   Ministry   Children   Career

      1 - _____   2 - _____   3 - _____   4 - _____   5 - _____

25. Define love and lust.

    Love is _____

    _____

    Lust is _____

    _____

26. Name the three major categories of temptation that come to all men.

    a. _____ b. _____ c. _____

27. Name the two "spiritual kingdoms."

    Kingdom of _____

    Kingdom of _____

28. When God created the Body of Christ, the Church, He created a magnificent organization.

    ___ True ___ False

29. What starts the maturation process in our lives? _____

30. Fame and greatness are synonymous.   ___ True ___ False

31. Children may not always _____ us, but they will always _____ us.

32. God has a pattern for victory. To acquire strategy, _____ is necessary. To obtain a victory, a

    _____ is required.

33. A man can do nothing more than sit in a pew year after year and be a completely fulfilled Christian.

    ___ True ___ False

34. Christians can discover their ministry gifts by serving others.   ___ True ___ False

35. A man reveals the condition of his heart by his _____ toward money.

36. You can compensate for not tithing by praying and asking God to bless your work regardless.

    ___ True ___ False

37. There is no such thing as good or positive stress. ___ True ___ False

38. The more _____ matter is able to withstand, the more valuable it becomes.

39. In Scripture, God demanded that His people often make treaties with their enemies.

    ___ True ___ False

40. Everything in life is under the power of choice. Once the choice is made, you become _____

    _____.

41. Because of a man's need to provide for his family, his reputation within his workplace is by far more

    important than his reputation at home. ___ True ___ False

42. A man's criteria for decision making should be what?

    a. _____   c. _____

    b. _____   d. _____

43. Habits can be developed by default or _____.

44. List the fruit of the Spirit.

    a. _____   d. _____   g. _____

    b. _____   e. _____   h. _____

    c. _____   f. _____   i. _____

45. Provide the Scriptural reference for the "fruit." *(give book and chapter)* _____

46. Name at least three things a father must provide.

    a. _____   b. _____   c. _____

47. To love as God loves, fathers must love:

    a. _____   b. _____   c. _____

48. It is not the father's responsibility to make all his children's decisions for them but to _____

    _____.

49. What can be life's greatest treasure? _____

50. Romance is the most important component of a successful marriage.   ___ True ___ False

51. It is far more important for businessmen to concentrate on locating new customers than on developing more friendships.   ___ True ___ False

52. Is it possible to still please God when we've sinned? If so, how? _____

53. I want to be a real man.   ___ True ___ False

54. Short essay: **In your own words,** explain what is meant by "faithfulness is the cornerstone of character."

    What does this have to do with being a real man? Use personal illustrations and examples from the book.

    _____

    _____

    _____

    _____

    _____

    _____

    _____

Name _____

Address _____

Address _____

Telephone a.m. _____ p.m. _____

The Final Exam is required to be "commissioned." Groups that commission graduates of the
MAJORING IN MEN™ course are listed on
www.EdColeLibrary.org

Basic Daily Bible Reading

Read Proverbs each morning for wisdom, Psalms each evening for courage. Make copies of this chart and keep it in your Bible to mark off as you read. If you are just starting the habit of Bible reading, be aware that longer translations or paraphrases (such as Amplified and Living) will take longer to read each day. As you start, it is okay to read only one of the chapters in Psalms each night, instead of the many listed. Mark your chart so you'll remember which ones you haven't read.

NOTE: The chronological chart following has the rest of the chapters of Psalms that are not listed here. By using both charts together, you will cover the entire book of Psalms.

Day of Month	Proverbs	Psalms	Day of Month	Proverbs	Psalms
1	1	1, 2, 4, 5, 6	18	18	82, 83, 84, 85
2	2	7, 8, 9	19	19	87, 88, 91, 92
3	3	10, 11, 12, 13, 14, 15	20	20	93, 94, 95, 97
4	4	16, 17, 19, 20	21	21	98, 99, 100, 101, 103
5	5	21, 22, 23	22	22	104, 108
6	6	24, 25, 26, 27	23	23	109, 110, 111
7	7	28, 29, 31, 32	24	24	112, 113, 114, 115, 117
8	8	33, 35	25	25	119:1-56
9	9	36, 37	26	26	119:57-112
10	10	38, 39, 40	27	27	119:113-176
11	11	41, 42, 43, 45, 46	28	28	120, 121, 122, 124, 130, 131, 133, 134
12	12	47, 48, 49, 50			
13	13	53, 55, 58, 61, 62	29	29	135, 136, 138
14	14	64, 65, 66, 67	30	30	139, 140, 141, 143
15	15	68, 69	31	31	144, 145, 146, 148, 150
16	16	70, 71, 73			
17	17	75, 76, 77, 81			

Chronological Annual Bible Reading

This schedule follows the events of the Bible chronologically and can be used with any translation or paraphrase of the Bible. Each day has an average of 77 verses of Scripture. If you follow this annually, along with your Daily Bible Reading, by your third year, you will recognize where you are and what is going to happen next. By your fifth year, you will understand the Scriptural background and setting for any reference spoken of in a message or book. At that point, the Word will become more like "meat" to you and less like "milk." Once you understand the basic stories and what happens on the surface, God can reveal to you the layers of meaning beneath. So, make copies of this chart to keep in your Bible and mark off as you read. And start reading—it's the greatest adventure in life!

Some notes:

1. Some modern translations don't have verses numbered (such as The Message), so they cannot be used with this chart. Also, if you are just starting the Bible, be aware that longer translations or paraphrases (such as Amplified and Living) tend to take longer to read each day.

2. The Daily Bible Reading chart covers the Proverbs and the chapters of Psalms that are not listed here. By using both charts together, you will cover the entire books of Psalms and Proverbs along with the rest of the Bible.

3. The chronology of Scripture is obvious in some cases, educated guesswork in others. The placement of Job, for example, is purely conjecture since there is no consensus among Bible scholars as to its date or place. For the most part, however, chronological reading helps the reader, since it places stories that have duplicated information, or prophetic utterances elsewhere in Scripture, within the same reading sequence.

HOW TO READ SCRIPTURE NOTATIONS:
Book chapter: verse. (Mark 15:44 means the book of Mark, chapter 15, verse 44.)
Book chapter; chapter (Mark 15; 16; 17 means the book of Mark, chapters 15, 16, 17.)
Books continue the same until otherwise noted. (2 Kings 22; 23:1-28; Jeremiah 20 means the book of 2 Kings, chapter 22, the book of 2 Kings, chapter 23, verses 1-28; then the book of Jeremiah, chapter 20.)

MAJORING IN MEN™

#	Date	Reading	#	Date	Reading	#	Date	Reading
1	Jan 1	Genesis 1; 2; 3	61	Mar 2	Numbers 32:28-42; 33			1 Chronicles 12:8-18; Psalm 57
2	Jan 2	Genesis 4; 5; 6	62	Mar 3	Numbers 34; 35; 36	117	Apr 27	1 Samuel 26; 27; 28; Psalms 54; 63
3	Jan 3	Genesis 7; 8; 9	63	Mar 4	Deuteronomy 1; 2	118	Apr 28	1 Samuel 29; 30; 31;
4	Jan 4	Genesis 10; 11; 12	64	Mar 5	Deuteronomy 3; 4			1 Chronicles 12:1-7; 12:19-22
5	Jan 5	Genesis 13; 14; 15; 16	65	Mar 6	Deuteronomy 5; 6; 7	119	Apr 29	1 Chronicles 10; 2 Samuel 1; 2
6	Jan 6	Genesis 17; 18; 19:1-29	66	Mar 7	Deuteronomy 8; 9; 10	120	Apr 30	2 Samuel 3; 4;
7	Jan 7	Genesis 19:30-38; 20; 21	67	Mar 8	Deuteronomy 11; 12; 13			1 Chronicles 11:1-9; 12:23-40
8	Jan 8	Genesis 22; 23; 24:1-31	68	Mar 9	Deuteronomy 14; 15; 16	121	May 1	2 Samuel 5; 6; 1 Chronicles 13; 14
9	Jan 9	Genesis 24:32-67; 25	69	Mar 10	Deuteronomy 17; 18; 19; 20	122	May 2	2 Samuel 22; 1 Chronicles 15
10	Jan 10	Genesis 26; 27	70	Mar 11	Deuteronomy 21; 22; 23	123	May 3	1 Chronicles 16; Psalm 18
11	Jan 11	Genesis 28; 29; 30:1-24	71	Mar 12	Deuteronomy 24; 25; 26; 27	124	May 4	2 Samuel 7; Psalms 96; 105
12	Jan 12	Genesis 30:25-35; 31	72	Mar 13	Deuteronomy 28	125	May 5	1 Chronicles 17; 2 Samuel 8; 9; 10
13	Jan 13	Genesis 32; 33; 34	73	Mar 14	Deuteronomy 29; 30; 31	126	May 6	1 Chronicles 18; 19; Psalm 60;
14	Jan 14	Genesis 35; 36	74	Mar 15	Deuteronomy 32; 33			2 Samuel 11
15	Jan 15	Genesis 37; 38; 39	75	Mar 16	Deuteronomy 34; Psalm 90;	127	May 7	2 Samuel 12; 13;
16	Jan 16	Genesis 40; 41			Joshua 1; 2			1 Chronicles 20:1-3; Psalm 51
17	Jan 17	Genesis 42; 43	76	Mar 17	Joshua 3; 4; 5; 6	128	May 8	2 Samuel 14; 15
18	Jan 18	Genesis 44; 45	77	Mar 18	Joshua 7; 8; 9	129	May 9	2 Samuel 16; 17; 18; Psalm 3
19	Jan 19	Genesis 46; 47; 48	78	Mar 19	Joshua 10; 11	130	May 10	2 Samuel 19; 20; 21
20	Jan 20	Genesis 49; 50; Exodus 1	79	Mar 20	Joshua 12; 13; 14	131	May 11	2 Samuel 22; 23:8-23
21	Jan 21	Exodus 2; 3; 4	80	Mar 21	Joshua 15; 16	132	May 12	1 Chronicles 20:4-8; 11:10-25;
22	Jan 22	Exodus 5; 6; 7	81	Mar 22	Joshua 17; 18; 19:1-23			2 Samuel 23:24-39; 24
23	Jan 23	Exodus 8; 9	82	Mar 23	Joshua 19:24-51; 20; 21	133	May 13	1 Chronicles 11:26-47; 21; 22
24	Jan 24	Exodus 10; 11; 12	83	Mar 24	Joshua 22; 23; 24	134	May 14	1 Chronicles 23; 24; Psalm 30
25	Jan 25	Exodus 13; 14; 15	84	Mar 25	Judges 1; 2; 3:1-11	135	May 15	1 Chronicles 25; 26
26	Jan 26	Exodus 16; 17; 18	85	Mar 26	Judges 3:12-31; 4; 5	136	May 16	1 Chronicles 27; 28; 29
27	Jan 27	Exodus 19; 20; 21	86	Mar 27	Judges 6; 7	137	May 17	1 Kings 1; 2:1-12; 2 Samuel 23:1-7
28	Jan 28	Exodus 22; 23; 24	87	Mar 28	Judges 8; 9	138	May 18	1 Kings 2:13-46; 3;
29	Jan 29	Exodus 25; 26	88	Mar 29	Judges 10; 11; 12			2 Chronicles 1:1-13
30	Jan 30	Exodus 27; 28; 29:1-28	89	Mar 30	Judges 13; 14; 15	139	May 19	1 Kings 5; 6; 2 Chronicles 2
31	Jan 31	Exodus 29:29-46; 30; 31	90	Mar 31	Judges 16; 17; 18	140	May 20	1 Kings 7; 2 Chronicles 3; 4
32	Feb 1	Exodus 32; 33; 34	91	Apr 1	Judges 19; 20	141	May 21	1 Kings 8; 2 Chronicles 5
33	Feb 2	Exodus 35; 36			*[You have completed 1/4 of the Bible!]*	142	May 22	1 Kings 9; 2 Chronicles 6; 7:1-10
34	Feb 3	Exodus 37; 38	92	Apr 2	Judges 21; Job 1; 2; 3	143	May 23	1 Kings 10:1-13; 2 Chronicles
35	Feb 4	Exodus 39; 40	93	Apr 3	Job 4; 5; 6			7:11-22; 8; 9:1-12; 1 Kings 4
36	Feb 5	Leviticus 1; 2; 3; 4	94	Apr 4	Job 7; 8; 9	144	May 24	1 Kings 10:14-29; 2 Chronicles
37	Feb 6	Leviticus 5; 6; 7	95	Apr 5	Job 10; 11; 12			1:14-17; 9:13-28; Psalms 72; 127
38	Feb 7	Leviticus 8; 9; 10	96	Apr 6	Job 13; 14; 15	145	May 25	Song of Solomon 1; 2; 3; 4; 5
39	Feb 8	Leviticus 11; 12; 13:1-37	97	Apr 7	Job 16; 17; 18; 19	146	May 26	Song of Solomon 6; 7; 8;
40	Feb 9	Leviticus 13:28-59; 14	98	Apr 8	Job 20; 21			1 Kings 11:1-40
41	Feb 10	Leviticus 15; 16	99	Apr 9	Job 22; 23; 24	147	May 27	Ecclesiastes 1; 2; 3; 4
42	Feb 11	Leviticus 17; 18; 19	100	Apr 10	Job 25; 26; 27; 28	148	May 28	Ecclesiastes 5; 6; 7; 8
43	Feb 12	Leviticus 20; 21; 22:1-16			[Accelerated Bible Reading Plan (from next pages)	149	May 29	Ecclesiastes 9; 10; 11; 12; 1 Kings
44	Feb 13	Leviticus 22:17-33; 23			finishes the entire Bible by this date!]			11:41-43; 2 Chronicles 9:29-31
45	Feb 14	Leviticus 24; 25	101	Apr 11	Job 29; 30; 31	150	May 30	1 Kings 12; 2 Chronicles 10; 11
46	Feb 15	Leviticus 26; 27	102	Apr 12	Job 32; 33; 34	151	May 31	1 Kings 13; 14; 2 Chronicles 12
47	Feb 16	Numbers 1; 2	103	Apr 13	Job 35; 36; 37	152	June 1	1 Kings 15: 2 Chronicles 13; 14; 15
48	Feb 17	Numbers 3; 4:1-20	104	Apr 14	Job 38; 39	153	June 2	1 Kings 16; 2 Chronicles 16; 17
49	Feb 18	Numbers 4:21-49; 5; 6	105	Apr 15	Job 40; 41; 42	154	June 3	1 Kings 17; 18; 19
50	Feb 19	Numbers 7	106	Apr 16	Ruth 1; 2; 3	155	June 4	1 Kings 20; 21
51	Feb 20	Numbers 8; 9; 10	107	Apr 17	Ruth 4; 1 Samuel 1; 2	156	June 5	1 Kings 22; 2 Chronicles 18
52	Feb 21	Numbers 11; 12; 13	108	Apr 18	1 Samuel 3; 4; 5; 6	157	June 6	2 Kings 1; 2;
53	Feb 22	Numbers 14; 15	109	Apr 19	1 Samuel 7; 8; 9			2 Chronicles 19; 20; 21:1-3
54	Feb 23	Numbers 16; 17	110	Apr 20	1 Samuel 10; 11; 12; 13	158	June 7	2 Kings 3; 4
55	Feb 24	Numbers 18; 19; 20	111	Apr 21	1 Samuel 14; 15	159	June 8	2 Kings 5; 6; 7
56	Feb 25	Numbers 21; 22	112	Apr 22	1 Samuel 16; 17	160	June 8	2 Kings 8; 9; 2 Chronicles 21:4-20
57	Feb 26	Numbers 23; 24; 25	113	Apr 23	1 Samuel 18; 19; Psalm 59	161	June 10	2 Chronicles 22; 23; 2 Kings 10; 11
58	Feb 27	Numbers 26; 27	114	Apr 24	1 Samuel 20; 21; Psalms 34; 56	162	June 11	Joel 1; 2; 3
59	Feb 28	Numbers 28; 29; 30	115	Apr 25	1 Samuel 22; 23; Psalms 52; 142	163	June 12	2 Kings 12; 13; 2 Chronicles 24
60	Mar 1	Numbers 31; 32:1-27	116	Apr 26	1 Samuel 24; 25;			

164	June 13	2 Kings 14; 2 Chronicles 25; Jonah 1
165	June 14	Jonah 2; 3; 4; Hosea 1; 2; 3; 4
166	June 15	Hosea 5; 6; 7; 8; 9; 10
167	June 16	Hosea 11; 12; 13; 14; 2 Kings 15:1-7
168	June 17	2 Kings 15:1-7; 2 Chronicles 26; Amos 1; 2; 3
169	June 18	Amos 4; 5; 6; 7
170	June 19	Amos 8; 9; 2 Kings 15:8-18; Isaiah 1
171	June 20	Isaiah 2; 3; 4; 2 Kings 15:19-38; 2 Chronicles 27
172	June 21	Isaiah 5; 6; Micah 1; 2; 3
173	June 22	Micah 4; 5; 6; 7; 2 Kings 16:1-18
174	June 23	2 Chronicles 28; Isaiah 7; 8
175	June 24	Isaiah 9; 10; 11; 12
176	June 25	Isaiah 13; 14; 15; 16
177	June 26	Isaiah 17; 18; 19; 20; 21
178	June 27	Isaiah 22; 23; 24; 25
179	June 28	Isaiah 26; 27; 28; 29
180	June 29	Isaiah 30; 31; 32; 33
181	June 30	Isaiah 34; 35; 2 Kings 18:1-8; 2 Chronicles 29
182	July 1	2 Chronicles 30; 31; 2 Kings 17:1-41; 2 Kings 16:19-20
		[You have completed 1/2 of the Bible!]
183	July 2	2 Kings 18:9-37; 2 Chronicles 32:1-19; Isaiah 36
184	July 3	2 Kings 19; 2 Chronicles 32:20-23; Isaiah 37
185	July 4	2 Kings 20; 21:1-18; 2 Chronicles 32:24-33; Isaiah 38; 39
186	July 5	2 Chronicles 33:1-20; Isaiah 40; 41
187	July 6	Isaiah 42; 43; 44
188	July 7	Isaiah 45; 46; 47; 48
189	July 8	Isaiah 49; 50; 51; 52
190	July 9	Isaiah 53; 54; 55; 56; 57
191	July 10	Isaiah 58; 59; 60; 61; 62
192	July 11	Isaiah 63; 64; 65; 66
193	July 12	2 Kings 21:19-26; 2 Chronicles 33:21-25; 34:1-7; Zephaniah 1; 2; 3
194	July 13	Jeremiah 1; 2; 3
195	July 14	Jeremiah 4; 5
196	July 15	Jeremiah 6; 7; 8
197	July 16	Jeremiah 9; 10; 11
198	July 17	Jeremiah 12; 13; 14; 15
199	July 18	Jeremiah 16; 17; 18; 19
200	July 19	Jeremiah 20; 2 Kings 22; 23:1-28
201	July 20	2 Chronicles 34:8-33; 35:1-19; Nahum 1; 2; 3
202	July 21	2 Kings 23:29-37; 2 Chronicles 35:20-27; 36:1-5; Jeremiah 22:10-17; 26; Habakkuk 1
203	July 22	Habakkuk 2; 3; Jeremiah 46; 47; 2 Kings 24:1-4; 2 Chronicles 36:6-7
204	July 23	Jeremiah 25; 35; 36; 45
205	July 24	Jeremiah 48; 49:1-33
206	July 25	Daniel 1; 2
207	July 26	Jeremiah 22:18-30; 2 Kings

208	July 27	24:5-20; 2 Chronicles 36:8-12; Jeremiah 37:1-2; 52:1-3; 24; 29 Jeremiah 27; 28; 23
209	July 28	Jeremiah 50; 51:1-19
210	July 29	Jeremiah 51:20-64; 49:34-39; 34:1-22
211	July 30	Ezekiel 1; 2; 3; 4
212	July 31	Ezekiel 5; 6; 7; 8
213	Aug 1	Ezekiel 9; 10; 11; 12
214	Aug 2	Ezekiel 13, 14, 15, 16:1-34
215	Aug 3	Ezekiel 16:35-63; 17; 18
216	Aug 4	Ezekiel 19; 20
217	Aug 5	Ezekiel 21; 22
218	Aug 6	Ezekiel 23; 2 Kings 25:1; 2 Chronicles 36:13-16; Jeremiah 39:1; 52:4; Ezekiel 24
219	Aug 7	Jeremiah 21; 22:1-9; 32; 30
220	Aug 8	Jeremiah 31; 33; Ezekiel 25
221	Aug 9	Ezekiel 29:1-16; 30; 31; 26
222	Aug 10	Ezekiel 27; 28; Jeremiah 37:3-21
223	Aug 11	Jeremiah 38; 39:2-10; 52:5-30
224	Aug 12	2 Kings 25:2-22; 2 Chronicles 36:17-21; Jeremiah 39:11-18; 40:1-6; Lamentations 1
225	Aug 13	Lamentations 2; 3
226	Aug 14	Lamentations 4; 5; Obadiah; Jeremiah 40:7-16
227	Aug 15	Jeremiah 41; 42; 43; 44; 2 Kings 25:23-26
228	Aug 16	Ezekiel 33:21-33; 34; 35; 36
229	Aug 17	Ezekiel 37; 38; 39
230	Aug 18	Ezekiel 32; 33:1-20; Daniel 3
231	Aug 19	Ezekiel 40; 41
232	Aug 20	Ezekiel 42; 43; 44
233	Aug 21	Ezekiel 45; 46; 47
234	Aug 22	Ezekiel 48; 29:17-21; Daniel 4
235	Aug 23	Jeremiah 52:31-34; 2 Kings 25:27-30; Psalms 44; 74; 79
236	Aug 24	Psalms 80; 85; 89
237	Aug 25	Psalms 102; 106
238	Aug 26	Psalms 123; 137; Daniel 7; 8
239	Aug 27	Daniel 5; 9; 6
240	Aug 28	2 Chronicles 36:22-23; Ezra 1; 2
241	Aug 29	Ezra 3; 4:1-5; Daniel 10; 11
242	Aug 30	Daniel 12; Ezra 4:6-24; 5; 6:1-13; Haggai 1
243	Aug 31	Haggai 2; Zechariah 1; 2; 3
244	Sept 1	Zechariah 4; 5; 6; 7; 8
245	Sept 2	Ezra 6:14-22; Psalm 78
246	Sept 3	Psalms 107; 116; 118
247	Sept 4	Psalms 125; 126; 128; 129; 132; 147
248	Sept 5	Psalm 149; Zechariah 9; 10; 11; 12; 13
249	Sept 6	Zechariah 14; Esther 1; 2; 3
250	Sept 7	Esther 4; 5; 6; 7; 8
251	Sept 8	Esther 9; 10; Ezra 7; 8
252	Sept 9	Ezra 9; 10; Nehemiah 1
253	Sept 10	Nehemiah 2; 3; 4; 5

254	Sept 11	Nehemiah 6; 7
255	Sept 12	Nehemiah 8; 9; 10
256	Sept 13	Nehemiah 11; 12
257	Sept 14	Nehemiah 13; Malachi
258	Sept 15	1 Chronicles 1; 2:1-35
259	Sept 16	1 Chronicles 2:36-55; 3, 4
260	Sept 17	1 Chronicles 5; 6:1-41
261	Sept 18	1 Chronicles 6:41-81; 7
262	Sept 19	1 Chronicles 8; 9
263	Sept 20	Matthew 1; 2; 3; 4
264	Sept 21	Matthew 5; 6
265	Sept 22	Matthew 7; 8
266	Sept 23	Matthew 9; 10
267	Sept 24	Matthew 11; 12
268	Sept 25	Matthew 13; 14
269	Sept 26	Matthew 15; 16
270	Sept 27	Matthew 17; 18; 19
271	Sept 28	Matthew 20; 21
272	Sept 29	Matthew 22; 23
273	Sept 30	Matthew 24; 25
		[You have completed 3/4 of the Bible!]
274	Oct 1	Matthew 26; 27; 28
275	Oct 2	Mark 1; 2
276	Oct 3	Mark 3; 4
277	Oct 4	Mark 5; 6
278	Oct 5	Mark 7; 8:1-26
279	Oct 6	Mark 8:27-38; 9
280	Oct 7	Mark 10; 11
281	Oct 8	Mark 12; 13
282	Oct 9	Mark 14
283	Oct 10	Mark 15; 16
284	Oct 11	Luke 1
285	Oct 12	Luke 2; 3
286	Oct 13	Luke 4; 5
287	Oct 14	Luke 6; 7:1-23
288	Oct 15	Luke 7:24-50; 8
289	Oct 16	Luke 9
290	Oct 17	Luke 10; 11
291	Oct 18	Luke 12; 13
292	Oct 19	Luke 14; 15
293	Oct 20	Luke 16; 17
294	Oct 21	Luke 18; 19
295	Oct 22	Luke 20; 21
296	Oct 23	Luke 22
297	Oct 24	Luke 23; 24:1-28
298	Oct 25	Luke 24:29-53; John 1
299	Oct 26	John 2; 3; 4:1-23
300	Oct 27	John 4:24-54; 5; 6:1-7
301	Oct 28	John 6:8-71; 7:1-21
302	Oct 29	John 7:22-53; 8
303	Oct 30	John 9; 10
304	Oct 31	John 11; 12:1-28
305	Nov 1	John 12:29-50; 13; 14
306	Nov 2	John 15; 16; 17
307	Nov 3	John 18; 19:1-24
308	Nov 4	John 19:25-42; 20; 21
309	Nov 5	Acts 1; 2
310	Nov 6	Acts 3; 4
311	Nov 7	Acts 5; 6
312	Nov 8	Acts 7

313	Nov 9	Acts 8; 9
315	Nov 11	Acts 10; 11
316	Nov 12	Acts 12; 13
317	Nov 13	Acts 14; 15; Galatians 1
318	Nov 14	Galatians 2; 3; 4
319	Nov 15	Galatians 5; 6; James 1
320	Nov 16	James 2; 3; 4; 5
321	Nov 17	Acts 16; 17
322	Nov 18	Acts 18:1-11; 1 Thessalonians 1; 2; 3; 4
323	Nov 19	1 Thessalonians 5; 2 Thessalonians 1; 2; 3
324	Nov 20	Acts 18:12-22; 19:1-22; 1 Corinthians 1
325	Nov 21	1 Corinthians 2; 3; 4; 5
326	Nov 22	1 Corinthians 6; 7; 8
327	Nov 23	1 Corinthians 9; 10; 11
328	Nov 24	1 Corinthians 12; 13; 14
329	Nov 25	1 Corinthians 15; 16
330	Nov 26	Acts 19:23-41; 20:1;

		2 Corinthians 1; 2
331	Nov 27	2 Corinthians 3; 4; 5
332	Nov 28	2 Corinthians 6; 7; 8; 9
333	Nov 29	2 Corinthians 10; 11; 12
334	Nov 30	2 Corinthians 13; Romans 1; 2
335	Dec 1	Romans 3; 4; 5
336	Dec 2	Romans 6; 7; 8
337	Dec 3	Romans 9; 10; 11
338	Dec 4	Romans 12; 13; 14
339	Dec 5	Romans 15; 16
340	Dec 6	Acts 20:2-38; 21
341	Dec 7	Acts 22; 23
342	Dec 8	Acts 24; 25; 26
343	Dec 9	Acts 27; 28
344	Dec 10	Ephesians 1; 2; 3
345	Dec 11	Ephesians 4; 5; 6
346	Dec 12	Colossians 1; 2; 3
347	Dec 13	Colossians 4; Philippians 1; 2
348	Dec 14	Philippians 3; 4; Philemon
349	Dec 15	1 Timothy 1; 2; 3; 4

350	Dec 16	1 Timothy 5; 6; Titus 1; 2
351	Dec 17	Titus 3; 2 Timothy 1; 2; 3
352	Dec 18	2 Timothy 4; 1 Peter 1; 2
353	Dec 19	1 Peter 3; 4; 5; Jude
354	Dec 20	2 Peter 1; 2; 3; Hebrews 1
355	Dec 21	Hebrews 2; 3; 4; 5
356	Dec 22	Hebrews 6; 7; 8; 9
357	Dec 23	Hebrews 10; 11
358	Dec 24	Hebrews 12; 13; 2 John; 3 John
359	Dec 25	1 John 1; 2; 3; 4
360	Dec 26	1 John 5; Revelation 1; 2
361	Dec 27	Revelation 3; 4; 5; 6
362	Dec 28	Revelation 7; 8; 9; 10; 11
363	Dec 29	Revelation 12; 13; 14; 15
364	Dec 30	Revelation 16; 17; 18; 19
365	Dec 31	Revelation 20; 21; 22

You have completed the entire Bible Congratulations!

NANCY CORBETT COLE CHARITIES

A portion of the proceeds from this book will be given to Nancy Corbett Cole Charities, serving the abused, addicted and abandoned. Internationally, "Nancy Corbett Cole Homes of Refuge" provide housing, vocational training and education for abused women and children. In the United States, help is ongoing on an individual and corporate basis.

Nancy Corbett Cole, "The Loveliest Lady in the Land," supported her husband, Edwin Louis Cole, in pursuing his life's mission for 54 years. Behind the scenes, she was a spiritual anchor and provider for many. Before her death in December, 2000, Nancy asked for the assurance that those for whom she had provided would not feel her absence. To fulfill that end, and for that purpose, Nancy Corbett Cole Charities were established.

By purchasing this book, you have helped society's under-served and less privileged members. If this book helped you, please consider sending a generous donation as well. Your one-time or continual support will help the helpless, heal the hurting and relieve the needy. Your gift is fully tax-deductible in the U.S. Send your compassionate contribution to:

Nancy Corbett Cole Charities
P. O. Box 92501
Southlake, TX 76092
USA
Thank you for your cheerful and unselfish care for others.

Watch for More Watercolor Books®

by terrific authors like –

Edwin Louis Cole

Steve Riggle

Nancy Corbett Cole

Karen Davis

Donald Ostrom

G. F. Watkins

Rod DePriest

Many more!

Southlake, Texas

ABOUT THE AUTHOR

Edwin Louis Cole, an internationally-acclaimed speaker, best-selling author and motivational lecturer, was known for his practical application of wisdom from Kingdom principles. Through his books, tapes and videos, the ministry to men continues to reach thousands of men worldwide, challenging them to fulfill their potential for true manhood, which is Christlikeness. His books have sold in the millions, including the landmark *Maximized Manhood*. Over five million people have studied his principles in the last fifty years. Considered "the father of the Christian men's movement," Edwin Louis Cole commissioned other men who now travel extensively worldwide to strengthen the ministry bases he founded under the divine guidance of the Holy Spirit.

Dr. Cole's lifetime body of work is being compiled at

www.EdColeLibrary.org

For more information, write:
Ed Cole™ Library
P.O. Box 92921
Southlake, TX 76092

Also by Edwin Louis Cole

Maximized Manhood
The Power of Potential
Real Man
Strong Men in Tough Times
Absolute Answers to Prodigal Problems
COURAGE
Winners Are Not Those Who Never Fail but Those Who NEVER QUIT!
Communication, Sex and Money
The Unique Woman
TREASURE
Irresistible Husband
Sexual Integrity

Study curriculum available for most books.
Answer keys for MAJORING IN MEN™ curriculum can be found at
www.watercolorbooks.com

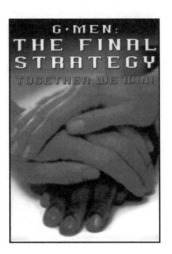

LEARN TO DISCIPLE MEN AND KEEP 70% OF YOUR CONVERTS IN YOUR CHURCH!

How do we "shut the back door" of the church and disciple the men God brings us? The G-MEN Strategy gives Christians purpose and a plan for spiritual growth, personal mentoring and evangelism. G-MEN are the *missing link* for building the Kingdom of God!

Designed and written by a pastor, these principles are flexible for any group or culture and easy to use. The G-MEN Strategy links the *problem* of discipling new converts with a *plan*. Mapped out step by step, these practical applications bring order, build the church and take the Gospel to the world. It's no theory. It's a time-tested plan of action that is world-changing revelation.

Can the G-MEN Strategy change the world? It already is!

Available in bookstores or contact www.watercolorbooks.com